DE HAVILLAND
A Pictorial Tribute

DE HAVILLAND
A Pictorial Tribute

Gordon Bain

Airlife
England

CONTENTS

Copyright © Gordon Bain 1992

British Library Cataloguing-in-Publication Data
A catalogue record for this book is available from the British Library.

ISBN 1 85310 144 3

First published by Airlife Publishing Ltd.

Printed in Singapore by Kyodo Printing Co. (S'pore) Pte Ltd.

Airlife Publishing Ltd.

101 Longden Road, Shrewsbury, England.

DH82A G-ACDC
Above: The Tiger Club's venerable DH82A G-ACDC seen here
in near silhouette near Redhill on 23 September 1987.

INTRODUCTION

Putting a book such as this together cannot be the work of just one person. Air to air photography is a team effort. A minimum of three people are involved in any particular sortie and all must pay close attention to their respective roles as the slightest mistake can lead to a dangerous situation and, possibly, no photographs.

The photographer has a picture in his mind of how the final photograph is to appear and it is his duty to communicate the idea to the pilot of the camera plane and the pilot of the subject aircraft during the pre-sortie briefing. Perhaps a cloudscape is required as a backdrop, perhaps a particular piece of scenery, perhaps certain lighting is required. If it's a formation shot then how is the formation to be put together. Who is formation leader? That is extremely important. What if something goes wrong — what do the individual pilots do? What are the hand signals? Radio frequencies? Safe speeds? Altitudes? Rendezvous points if flying from different airfields?

The pilots themselves must be good steady types — ham-fistedness is not wanted.

The photographer is just the guy holding the camera — he can only photograph what he sees through the viewfinder. The real experts are the pilots flying the aircraft, especially the chap in the subject aircraft. He has by far the most work to do. It has been my great pleasure to have flown with many different pilots in order to produce this book. All have been of differing experience ranging from PPLs through airline pilots to military and test pilots. The common thread holding them all together was their flying ability. If it was not for that ability the photographs in this book would not have been possible.

Many people have given their time and effort to help produce this book. Max Ward delayed delivery of his Fox Moth to the Canadian Transport Museum, Ottawa, so that I could take photographs for inclusion in the book. Mike and Mary Kimbrell made a total stranger feel like one of the family when the author arrived in Seattle to photograph his DH84 Dragon. John King flew the author around New Zealand in his Auster to get various photographs and was, generally, of tremendous help. Likewise, Watt Martin flew me around Ontario to get various shots and arranged for some aircraft to be flown into his strip at Milton just for the camera. Colonel Hans Rudolph Haberli put, what seemed to be, half of the Swiss Air Force at my disposal to get shots of the world's last operational Vampires. John and Jenny Pothecary have helped countless times with many air to air sessions (not just with de Havilland types) and it was Brian Dunlop who helped me on my way in the early days of my aerial photography. There have been many others about whom I could write. All, in Uncle Roger's words, are Total Aviation People. All are DH people. This book is for them. I hope they enjoy it.

Unfortunately it is not possible to name everyone who has contributed to this book but I would especially like to acknowledge the help of:

Air Commodore David L. Bywater; Sqdn. Ldr. John Taylor; John and Jenny Pothecary; Peter Harrison; Malcolm Blows; Dave Clarke; Chris Foss; Col. H. R. Haberli, Swiss Air Force; Mike and Mary Kimbrell; Brian Woodford; John King; Watt Martin; Max Ward; George Neal; Charles Masefield; Mike Brown (BAe); David Ogilvy; Ron Souch; Aer Lingus; Brian Dunlop; Simon Myatt; Stuart McKay; Richard Dent; Andy Stibbs; Dougal Mann; Lt. Cmdr. Chris Hill; Lt. Cmdr. Ned Stone; Lt. Cmdr. Tom Mason; Tim Williams; John Davis; Mike Vaisey; Paul and Andrew Wood; Tony Haig-Thomas; Angus McVitie and John Parkhouse.

Those not mentioned here are acknowledged through the rest of the book. My thanks to all of you.

DE HAVILLAND

by Gordon Bain

Born on 27 July 1882 Geoffrey de Havilland, son of Rev Charles de Havilland, had always been interested in things mechanical. He had been a pupil at Oakfield in Rugby and, later, at St Edwards School, Oxford. A three year mechanical engineering course followed at the Crystal Palace Engineering School commencing in 1900. At the end of his course his project was to build a petrol driven engine which he duly fitted to a cycle frame to provide him with transport to and from the family home in the rectory at Crux Easton near Newbury, Berkshire.

During the following three years he worked for Williams and Robinson of Rugby. Whilst there he designed and built his own petrol driven engine. After a further year in the employ of the Wolsey Tool and Motor Car Company he joined the Motor Omnibus Construction Company, as a designer, at Moorgate and then at Walthamstow.

Whilst at Walthamstow he was introduced to a young man called Frank T. Hearle who worked for Vanguard Omnibus Company. Both young men had a common interest in the new found sport of aviating.

De Havilland decided that he wanted to build his own aeroplane but to do so he needed finance. This was partly provided by his grandfather to the tune of £500. Further finance was to be provided by Mr Knowles of the Iris Motor Company of Willesden but he had second thoughts about the investment and he decided to withdraw from the scheme. This left Geoffrey in a predicament as £500 was totally insufficient to produce the aeroplane. Explaining this to his grandfather he was advanced another £500. This £1,000 was to have been de Havilland's bequest on his grandfather's death. The name of de Havilland was now set on its historic path in the world of aviation.

The first job to be tackled with the new aeroplane was the design of a new engine. The engine was to be a horizontally opposed, watercooled, four cylinder machine of 4,950cc displacement giving around 40–50hp at 1,500rpm. The engine was built by the Iris Motor Company at a cost of £250.

In the meantime de Havilland and Frank Hearle, destined to marry de Havilland's sister Ione in 1914, rented a workshop in Fulham in order to build their aeroplane, a biplane with a canard foreplane and a rear mounted stabiliser driven by twin propellers and powered by a single de Havilland designed engine.

On completion the aircraft was taken to Seven Barrows on the Hampshire Downs and, after many delays, a flight was attempted in December 1908. Although there was daylight under the wheels the flight came to a rapid and abrupt end when the port wing spar failed — fortunately without injury to the fledgling pilot.

Learning from this accident a second aircraft was built and, on 10 September 1910, was flown successfully at Seven Barrows. After further

Left: A de Havilland formation of DH82A, DH83C and DH87B flown, respectively, by Ian Houlihan, Colin Dodds and Peter Thorn. All three aircraft are owned by Victor Gauntlett and were shot over Sussex on 12 May 1991.

flights the aircraft was taken to Farnborough where it was flown on 14 January 1911. The War Office bought the aircraft for £400. At Farnborough the aircraft was called the FE1 (for Farman Experimental) and Geoffrey de Havilland gained his Royal Aero Club Aviators Certificate, No.53, on the aircraft on 7 February 1911. The FE1 subsequently crashed on 15 August 1911.

By now Geoffrey had joined the Army Aircraft Factory at Farnborough. This became the Royal Aircraft Factory and then, in 1918, the Royal Aircraft Establishment finally becoming the Royal Aerospace Establishment in 1988.

In 1912 he joined the reserve of the newly formed Royal Flying Corps as a 2nd Lieutenant.

Shortly before the Great War of 1914–18 the now Captain de Havilland was persuaded by Mr George Holt Thomas to leave the Royal Aircraft Factory and join him as Chief Designer at the Aircraft Manufacturing Company, where he worked throughout the War being responsible for the DH2, through to the DH9.

With the immediate post-war cutbacks the Aircraft Manufacturing Company, or AIRCO as it had become known, was sold to the Birmingham Small Arms Company early in 1920. But Air transport was not yet ready to take off and the aviation side of AIRCO was closed down almost immediately while BSA used the factory for other purposes.

After this bout of asset-stripping Geoffrey de Havilland decided that aviation did have a future and that he wanted to be part of it.

Investment proved to be forthcoming from various sources, including George Holt Thomas on the proviso that the Chairman of the proposed new firm should be A. E. Turner who had been the finance director of AIRCO. This was agreed to and de Havilland himself made an initial investment of some £3,000. The design and manufacturing rights for various projects were bought from BSA and, on 25 September 1920, the de Havilland Aircraft Company was formed. Joining de Havilland in the venture were the now famous names of C. C. Walker, appointed Chief Engineer; Frank T. Hearle, General Manager; W. E. Nixon, secretary and F. E. N. St Barbe as Sales Manager. All were appointed directors of the new firm. Also joining, as assistant designer, was a promising young man named Arthur E. Hagg. Business was set up in a small field at Stag Lane, Edgware. Those early days were not easy, however, and sales were slack.

Two events of great importance to the future of the Company happened in 1921. R. E. Bishop was employed as a designer but of more immediate importance was an order from Mr Alan S. Butler for a three seat touring aircraft to his own specification. He subsequently invested in the Company by purchasing the Stag Lane site from its owners Messrs Warren and Smiles. But for these latter events it is likely that the fledgling company would have folded and the future of aviation would have taken a rather different path.

The aircraft which saved de Havilland was the DH37. Two were built in 1922. As a result of his association with the de Havilland Aircraft Company Alan S. Butler was Chairman from February 1923 and held this post until his retirement in June 1950. Thanks to his efforts de Havilland went on to achieve great heights in all aspects of aviation with a legacy leading on to the merger with the Hawker Siddeley Group in 1960 and continuing to this day under the flag of British Aerospace PLC.

Alan S. Butler died on 24 May 1987 aged 88 years.

Geoffrey de Havilland was knighted in 1944 for services to aviation. He died, in retirement, on 26 May 1965 one of the greatest pioneers of aviation.

This book is primarily concerned with those DH aircraft currently in existence and, in the main, in flying condition.

THE DH51

The DH51 was an early attempt to produce a cheap and comparatively simple aircraft which many people could afford to operate and buy. It was a two bay biplane using standard de Havilland construction methods. The fuselage was ply covered and the wings were fabric covered with differential ailerons on the bottom mainplanes. The aircraft could seat three with the pilot in the rear cockpit and two passengers in the front in tandem. A sliding decking covered the front passenger seat if only one passenger was carried. Thirty gallons of fuel was carried in a centre section tank in the top wing, giving a range of 360 miles. The intended engine for the DH51 was the RAF 1A of 90 hp.

The first flight of the prototype, G-EBIM c/n 100, took place on 1 July 1924, with Geoffrey de Havilland at the controls.

Difficulties arose with the Air Ministry over the RAF 1A engine, however, as it had only single ignition. A CofA would not be forthcoming unless the engine was modified to have dual ignition and a ten hour trouble free test run completed. This was going to prove expensive, an estimate being in the vicinity of £100, a lot of money then. A solution was found in the 80 hp Renault engine. This was modified by Major F. B. Halford of the Aircraft Disposal Company (Airdisco) to produce 120 hp and the aircraft was offered with this powerplant. Unfortunately it was no longer cheap enough to be affordable and only three aircraft were ever built.

The only remaining aircraft of the three is the last to be built, G-EBIR c/n 102, now in the hands of the Shuttleworth Collection at Old Warden airfield, Bedfordshire.

The aircraft was built for John Carberry and completed in 1925. It was shipped to Mombasa, Kenya, on 17 September 1925 and flew there for the first time on 4 April 1926. Although registered G-EBIR it did not carry these marks until 1973!

The aircraft was bought, in June 1928, by G. Skinner, A. Hughes and Tom Campbell-Black, later to achieve fame in a DH88, and subsequently it was to be re-registered G-KAA on 10 September 1928. Once again these marks were not carried. On 3 January 1929 the aircraft became VP-KAA under the revised Kenyan registration system. This time the aircraft did carry its new marks and did so until its arrival back in the UK, in 1965 in

DH51 G-EBIR c/n 102

Overleaf: It can be fairly said that, although only three of the type were ever built, the DH51 represented the start of the 'Moth' lineage and, therefore, the future good fortunes of the de Havilland Company. Only the third aircraft built now survives. G-EBIR, 'Miss Kenya', is now in the care of the Shuttleworth Trust based at Old Warden airfield, Bedfordshire.

These photographs were taken on 24 September 1989 just prior to the start of the 'Shuttleworth Pageant', a display of the Trust's aircraft held on the first Sunday of September every year. Pilot for the occasion was one of the Collection's regular display pilots, and former 'Moth' collector, Tony Haig-Thomas.

the hold of a RAF Beverley. Having now been acquired by the Shuttleworth Trust the airframe was stripped and refurbished by apprentices at Hawker Siddeley's factory at Hawarden, Cheshire. The engine was similarly treated by Rolls Royce at Leavesden.

The aircraft made its first post restoration flight, finally wearing the marks of G-EBIR, on 15 March 1973 at the hands of Air Commodore Allen Wheeler. Now named Miss Kenya she flies regularly at the air days at its home, Old Warden.

DH51 G-EBIR

Above: The 120hp of the Airdisco engine requires a four bladed propeller to absorb the power. 'Miss Kenya' was photographed at Old Warden during the 'Shuttleworth Pageant' in September 1988.

THE DH53

Also housed with the Shuttleworth Trust at Old Warden is the prototype DH53 'Humming Bird', G-EBHX. Although the aircraft is essentially airworthy, and the engine is run during the air days, to taxi the aircraft around Old Warden aerodrome the decision has been taken, for the time being, not to fly the aircraft. This decision follows an engine failure and a forced landing on 31 August 1980.

The DH53 was the de Havilland entry for the 1923 light aircraft trials at Lympne, Kent. Construction followed normal de Havilland practice with a plywood covered fuselage having spruce longerons. The wings were of two spar construction and fabric covered with differential ailerons. Bracing was in the form of solid spruce V struts, in compression, attached to the top longerons. The wings were arranged to fold. The engine was a Douglas 750cc motor cycle engine. It was this engine that was to prove one of the aircraft's greatest handicaps as its reliability left a deal to be desired. Despite the problem with the engine the two aircraft entered for the Lympne trials put up a good show in the hands of Major Hemmings and Hubert Broad.

On return to Stag Lane the Douglas engine was replaced by a Blackburn Tomtit two cylinder inverted V engine of 698cc and delivering 26hp. The fuel capacity was increased from its original two gallons by fitting another tank in the shape of the headrest.

On 8 December 1923 the prototype was marked as G-EBHX, renamed 'L'Oiseau Mouche' and flown, by Alan Cobham, to the Brussels Aero Show via Croydon and Lympne.

After passing through the hands of F. J. V. Holmes and E. W. Kennet it was found in the back garden of a house at Eastrey, Kent, in 1955 by Squadron Leader L. A. Jackson of the Shuttleworth Trust. It was minus the starboard aileron, engine mounting, tailplane, controls and tanks. As the drawings no longer existed these were designed and built by the de Havilland Technical School. Fitted with an A.B.C. Scorpion of 35hp it flew again on 4 August 1960 at Hatfield and was, shortly afterwards, handed over to the Shuttleworth Trust.

In all fifteen DH53s were built.

DH53 G-EBHX c/n 98

Right: Chris Morris, Chief Engineer of the Shuttleworth Collection, blows away the cobwebs as he runs the A.B.C. Scorpion of the protoype DH53 Humming Bird. G-EBHX, at Old Warden during the summer of 1987. Although maintained in flying condition the decision was taken not to fly this sole remaining aircraft after an engine failure and forced landing on 31 August 1980.

THE DH60 MOTH

Flight for 5 March 1925 stated that 'From whichever point of view one regards it, the de Havilland "Moth" must be considered a very fine little aeroplane' — 'and it is hoped to be, although naturally this still has to be proved, one of the most reliable little machines of modern times. If orders are forthcoming in sufficient numbers, one can see a very bright future for the de Havilland Moth'. Little did the writer of those words realise just how bright the future was to be.

Although it won no prizes, the tiny DH53 put up a very creditable showing at the 1923 Lympne trials. Geoffrey de Havilland realised, however, that the specifications for the trials were always going to result in aircraft of mediocre performance and any aircraft developed to these specifications would not be rugged enough for normal club use. The 1924 trials were for a two seat aircraft with an engine of less than 1,100cc! This would lead to a very light structure. The engines were also of dubious reliability.

De Havilland decided to go along a somewhat different path by scaling down the company's DH51. The result was the DH60 'Moth'. The name was inspired by Captain de Havilland's reputation as a lepidopterist. The engine was specially designed by Major F. B. Halford of Airdisco. He took half of the cylinders from the firm's 120hp eight cylinder V-type engine (itself derived from the old 80hp Renault) mated the four cylinders to a new crankcase and thus was born the Cirrus 1 upright engine which delivered 60hp for a weight of 290lbs.

The aircraft was a single bay biplane of standard spruce and plywood construction, fabric covered, with tandem seating for two.

The fuselage was built around a square section formed by four longerons with a rounded upper decking, the whole being covered with plywood. The Cirrus engine was fitted in an upright position.

A fifteen gallon fuel tank, in an aerofoil section, formed the centre section of the upper wing. This tank was supported on four upright and two sloping bracing struts. The wings themselves were of two spar construction, the spars being spindled from the solid. There was one set of interplane struts per side and the wings were braced by streamline flying wires. Differential ailerons were fitted to the bottom wings only. The wings were made to fold about the rear spar with jury struts to support the inboard ends when folded. Total width when folded was nine feet eight inches which not only saved room in a hangar but allowed a considerable reduction in the inevitable hangar fees.

DH60G G-ABEV c/n 1823
Left: Rebuilt by Ron Souch at Hamble, 'BEV is now owned by Brian Woodford's Wessex Aviation and Transport Ltd. at Chalmington, Dorset. Previous identities have been N4203E and CH-217, later becoming HB-OKI under the revised Swiss register.

Former RAF Jaguar pilot, Nigel Reid flew the aircraft near Old Warden for the photograph on 18 August 1989.

Empty weight was 764 lbs and loaded weight was 1,250 lbs. Maximum speed was 90 mph on the 60 hp Cirrus.

The first Moth built was G-EBKT and it took to the air for the first time, with Geoffrey de Havilland at the controls, on 22 February 1925 at Stag Lane.

Efforts by Sir Sefton Brancker, Director of Civil Aviation, resulted in five Moth-equipped clubs being set up. The first of these, The Lancashire Aero Club at Woodford, took delivery of their first Moth, G-EBLR (c/n 184) on 21 July 1925, having been flown there by A. J. Cobham. This aircraft crashed at Hale, Cheshire, on 12 June 1927. On 29 August 1925 the eighth machine built, G-EBLV (c/n 188) was delivered to the Club. This venerable aircraft is now maintained in an airworthy condition by British Aerospace at Hatfield where it is taken out on high days and holidays to have the wind blow through its wires and lift it in to its natural environment.

'EBKT flew, initially, with an unbalanced rudder and the exhaust pipe on the starboard side of the fuselage. It was soon after modified to have a horn balanced rudder and the exhaust on the port side. This last modification was to be a feature of almost all the DH60 Moths produced and contributed greatly to the comfort of the occupants by providing warmth in the cockpit on cold days. One just had to remember not to hold on to it when evacuating the cockpit!

Twenty Moths were built in that first year of production, 1925.

DH60 Moths were built, under licence, in Australia and Finland as well as at Stag Lane and were variously engined with Cirrus 1, II, III, Cirrus Hermes I and the Armstrong Siddeley Genet to produce the Genet Moth, some of which were operated by the RAF's Central Flying School.

A single Hermes powered DH60X, G-EBWD, still flies with the Shuttleworth Collection at Old Warden.

By 1926 the success of the Moth was quite apparent and the demand was considerable. The potential limiting factor was the availability of the Cirrus engine. De Havilland felt some unease about the engine supply situation and decided that the company should undertake manufacture of its own engine for the DH60. Major Frank Halford was approached again and asked to design a completely new engine. Design work commenced in October 1926 and the first engine ran in July 1927. This engine was called the DH Gipsy 1 and it was to revolutionise the DH60 series. It was rated at 100 hp at 2,100 rpm.

The first production engine flew in DH60X, G-EBQH. This aircraft took part in the 1928 King's Cup Air Race with G-EBYK and 'YZ. It was the first public appearance of the new DH60G 'Gipsy Moth' and it was G-EBYZ which won the race at 105 mph. The de Havilland publicity machine was finding its feet in those early days and such coups as this helped its efforts immensely over the coming years. The next great piece of publicity for this engine/airframe combination was the 'sealed engine test'.

A standard Gipsy 1 fitted to G-EBTD was flown with only routine maintenance for 600 hours after being sealed by the AID between 29 December 1928 and 24 September 1929. Fifty one thousand miles were covered and the aircraft was flown by many different pilots. At the end of the test period the replacement parts cost the sum of only £7–2s–11d.

De Havillands were really getting into their stride now. Moths were appearing in every corner of the globe. The cost to fly away from Stag Lane was £650. Further licence production was granted to 'Aeroplanes

DH60 Cirrus Moth G-EBLV c/n 188

Below: Number eight off the DH60 production line, G-EBLV was delivered to the Lancashire Aero Club at Woodford, Cheshire, on 29 August 1925, having been flown there from Stag Lane by one Alan Cobham. Passing through the hands of various owners its penultimate operator was Mr John Jefferson who purchased it in 1938 for £185. In the meantime de Havillands were trying to trace the whereabouts of the prototype DH60 Moth, G-EBKT, but had discovered that it had recently crashed with some of the parts being used to repair G-EBLV after it, too, had pranged at Castle Bromwich on 5 February 1939.

'EBLV was offered to de Havillands for the price that Mr Jefferson had paid for it — plus the sum of £25 'fine' for the RAF Benevolent Fund for their tardiness in trying to preserve such a famous aircraft as the one which started the light aviation movement.

Stored through the war years 'EBLV was restored to airworthiness in the early '50s by apprentices of the DH Technical School at Panshangar.

Sharing a hangar with BAe125s and BAe146s 'EBLV now resides under the care of British Aerospace at Hatfield from where the aircraft was flown for this photograph on 20 August 1989. Pilot for the occasion was Charles Masefield, Managing Director of BAe Civil Division, with his son, Fraser, occupying the front seat.

Morane Saulnier' at Villacoublay, France, and to 'The Moth Corporation' at Lowell, Massachusetts, USA.

The DH60M Moth (Metal Moth) was put into production in 1928. These aircraft, as the name suggests, had a fuselage of welded steel tube. Although this added 62 lbs to the empty weight it had advantages such as simpler maintenance. The DH60M could easily be distinguished from its wooden fuselaged forebears by the somewhat rounder appearance given by the stringers.

DH60X Hermes Moth G-EBWD

Above: Originally powered by a 65 hp Cirrus 1 engine 'BWD now has a 105 hp Hermes II fitted.

Built in 1928 it was acquired by Richard Shuttleworth in 1932. It has lived at Old Warden Aerodrome ever since and qualifies as having been based at the same airfield longer than any other aeroplane in history.

Above: Watt Martin flying his DH60G, CF-AAA, near his strip
at Milton, Ontario.

DH60G G-ABEV c/n 1823
Previous page: *De rigeur* for the English country gentleman was the Moth on the lawn with the Rolls Royce Silver Ghost in front of a virginia creeper-clad manor. It could be the 1930s but it's Brian Woodford's DH60G in front of Chalmington Manor during the autumn of 1988.

DH60G G-ATBL c/n 1917
Above: 'TBL was a Stag Lane-built machine which was exported to Switzerland as HB-OBA. It returned to England in 1965 as G-ATBL, flown by Edward Eves. Later refurbished by Cliff Lovell it was sold to Tony Haig-Thomas to join his large collection of DH types. It was eventually sold to Michael Vaisey who is seen flying it on 28 June 1981 near Old Warden airfield.

DH60G G-AAOR/EM.01 c/n 1075
Right: Wandering through an old olive grove near Lerida, Spain, in 1980 John Pothecary came across an old shed. Lying inside was a crate containing four lower mainplanes for a DH60G along with fin, rudder, tailplane and elevators. Nearby lay a fuselage with engine and a burnt out centre section. The crate was stamped 'May 1940' and seemed for all the world to have been lying there since that date.
The history of the aircraft is obscure but it is known that it was once registered EC-AAO.
After having the remains shipped back to England a five year restoration started. Period registration G-AAOR was obtained and the Moth took to the air again in 1986 in the probable colours of a flying training school of the Spanish Government of 1936. Christened 'La Madrina' the aircraft was photographed on 22 September 1986 with John flying.

DH60G G-AAOR/30-76 c/n 1075

Above: Still under the ownership of John Pothecary, DH60G
G-AAOR is seen here repainted as 30-76 of the Spanish
Nationalist Air Force of the 1930s. The shot was taken on 21
September 1989.

DH60G CF-AAA c/n 1840

Right: This is the second aircraft to carry the marks CF-AAA,
the first being a DH60M, the Canadian registration system
allowing reallocation.

Built in 1931 it was registered to W. L. Handley as G-ABJJ,
receiving its C. of A. on 28 March 1931. The aircraft passed
through the ownership of H. H. Johnson at Baginton, C. W. R.
Gleeson at Castle Bromwich and W. Adams at Yeadon, until it
was impressed into RAF service as BK842 on 10 September
1940 and sent to 39MU.

At the end of the war it was sent to 5MU for disposal. In
December 1945 it was sold to the Oxford Flying Club at
Kidlington and then, re-registered G-ABJJ on 19 February
1946, it passed to Airtraining (Oxford) Ltd. with a new C. of A.
issued on 1 May 1946.

'BJJ passed through the hands of various owners until it was
sold to George Neal, a DH (Canada) test pilot. George had the
aircraft rebuilt to its current standard. Now registered
CF-AAA it was bought by Watt Martin in August 1978 and is
now kept at Watt's farm strip south of Milton, Ontario. This
photograph was taken, near Milton, on 17 May 1989 with Watt
flying.

Watt Martin's restoration abilities in the cockpit of his DH60M
CF-AAJ shortly before her first post restoration flight.

G-AAWO/G-ANDM/G-BFHH

Overleaf: Floating along on a beautiful summer's day is
DH60G G-AAWO flown by Nigel Reid leading Tiger Moth's
G-ANDM, flown by Geoff Green, and G-BFHH, flown by
Martin Gambrell. Shot during the Moth Club rally at Woburn
Abbey on 19 August 1984.

DH60GMW G-AAMY c/n 86

Below: Built by the Moth Corporation at Lowell, Massachusetts, airframe number 86 was allocated the registration NC585M before being bought by Cliff Lovell for restoration. It flew in England for a while as N585M but was finally allocated the period marks G-AAMY on 2 May 1980. The aircraft was eventually bought by Roger Fiennes to be kept at Headcorn, Kent.

Right: Badge of the Moth Aircraft Corporation, Lowell, Massachusetts.

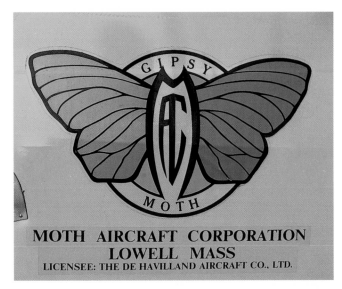

MOTH AIRCRAFT CORPORATION
LOWELL MASS
LICENSEE: THE DE HAVILLAND AIRCRAFT CO., LTD.

DH60M G-AANV c/n 13

Above: Commencing in 1929 a total of 40 DH60Ms were assembled by Aeroplanes Morane-Saulnier at Villacoublay, France, from parts sent out from the Stag Lane factory.

This aircraft was registered F-AJNY in 1930. Subsequent history is not known but it was in Switzerland before the war as HB-OBU. In 1968 it was grounded by the Swiss authorities as the rib stitching was disintegrating. It remained stored at

Bad Ragaz airfield, south east of Zurich, until its then owner Raoul Borner died. The remains were acquired by Ron Souch in June 1983 for a rebuild at Hamble flying again, as G-AANV, in June 1984 with a Gipsy 1 for power.

The new owner was former Concorde captain Derek Elliss who is seen here flying the aircraft on 6 July 1984, during the PFA rally at Cranfield.

DH60M G-AAMX c/n 125

Right: Built in the USA, by the Moth Corporation, this DH60M was originally registered as NC926M in 1929 and then written off in 1930 — a seemingly brief career. NC926M passed through various hands during the following years and was gradually stripped of various useful bits.

During 1983 R. John Parkhouse, Managing Director of the Army Weapons Division of British Aerospace, was in the process of building a Luton Minor when, in his own words, he found himself in need of a few personal medical modifications', the upshot of which was a restriction placed on his licence in that he could only fly P1 if another licensed pilot accompanied him. The Luton Minor, being a one holer, was no longer a suitable project.

Around this time a 'Basket case' Gipsy Moth was advertised for sale in *Flight International* and, after a variety of phone calls, John bought the mortal remains of NC926M and had them transported to Stevenage. A work schedule was prepared under the auspices of the Popular Flying Association's John Walker.

Many people in the restoration business helped with the rebuild including Cathy O'Brian and Tim Moore of Skysport Engineering who took on the task of repairing the steel tube fuselage, Ben Cooper who made the new wing spars and rib sets, Ron and Ivor Souch took on the Gipsy 1 engine which, when obtained, was sitting in a pool of oily water and was considered to be scrap. The BAe Apprentices School at Lostock rebuilt the undercarriage while Peter Jackson and Mike Vaisey came up with much information and many 'bits'. Recovering was aided and abetted by Andy Preslant.

A period registration was obtained from the CAA. In the '20s and '30s whole batches of registrations were allocated to manufacturers but the last three in the G-AAMA–MZ sequence were not taken up as those three aircraft went straight to a foreign country and did not carry their British marks. 'MY had already been taken by Cliff Lovell for his immaculate American Moth and so John chose G-AAMX.

The first engine runs were carried out at Hatfield on 25 July 1987. After some ground running the date for the first flight was set for Saturday 1 August 1987. At the controls was John and his old friend Des Penrose, a former Trident test pilot. This trip was comparatively short as a rear cylinder tappet adjuster was not all that it should be leading to a smoky trail from that lovely long Gipsy exhaust. A rummage around Mike Vaisey's box of bits produced a new one and, after some further ground running, 'MX took to the air again.

Sunday 16 August saw John at Hatfield with 'MX and Charles Masefield with the Cirrus Moth G-EBLV. Together they took off and headed towards the Moth Club meeting at Woburn where the Moth was put on public display for the first time.

John has now retired and lives at Rottingdean, Sussex. 'MX lives close by at Shoreham airfield from where this photograph was taken on 25 August 1989 when John was accompanied by Malcolm Blows.

DH60M G-AADR c/n 148

Right: Built by the Moth Aircraft Corporation at Lowell, Massachusetts and now owned by Hamish Moffatt, DH60M G-AADR sits under a stormy sky during the 1988 Moth Club Rally at Woburn Abbey. Originally registered NC939M the aircraft is now kept near Hereford.

DH60M G-AAHY c/n 1362

Below: Built in the UK in 1937, this airframe was sold in Switzerland as CH-480 (later HB-AFI). A rebuild was completed by Ron Souch, at Hamble, in 1987 after which the aircraft was allotted the period marks G-AAHY and was painted in the red, black and silver colours of the Brooklands Flying Club and sold to Ian White.

In 1987 Richard Parker, of Denham, purchased the aircraft but sold it again in 1988 to help finance the purchase of a Spitfire. The new owner was Michael Vaisey, former owner of DH60G G-ATBL. The aircraft is now kept at Old Warden airfield.

This photograph was taken on 26 September 1987 with Peter Kynsey in command near Denham.

DH60M(R) ZK-AEJ c/n 1542

Below: Built in 1930 as G-AAXG this aircraft was modified specially for Alan S. Butler for the Round Europe 'Challenge de Tourisme Internationale'.

As the aircraft was specifically built for racing it featured a number of modifications compared to a standard DH60M. The engine, a Gipsy II of 120hp, was lowered by two inches and a new set of cowlings made for improved streamlining. The exhaust was rerouted below the fuselage rather than along the port side. The centre section rear vertical struts were replaced by wires whilst the new front struts met on the centre line in front of the front cockpit which was fitted with a transparent canopy for racing. A new streamlined fuel tank was fitted in the centre section of the top wing with a supplementary 15 gallon tank in the front cockpit.

Wooden formers were fitted to the rear fuselage to give a rounder shape and to enclose the exposed control wires to the elevator and rudder.

These modifications paid off as Alan Butler achieved second place in the 1930 King's Cup Air Race at 129.7mph. After that race it was sold to Edouard A. Bret of Mougins, France, who flew it to victory, as F-AJZB, in the Coupe Zenith race around France in 1930.

The aircraft was sold to the Hon Brian Lewis in 1933 and, shortly afterwards, to H. R. A. Kidston, a Sub-Lieutenant in the Royal Navy, who had it shipped to New Zealand as ZK-AEJ.

The aircraft has been the subject of an extensive rebuild by New Zealand Moth expert Temple Martin for its current owner Gerald Grocott. The first flight after restoration took place on 1 July 1987.

The aircraft is almost as it was originally when owned by Alan Butler. Obvious differences are the 'doughnut' wheels instead of the slim, high pressure tyres, the style of cockpit canopy and the registration, although ZK-AEJ has been worn for many more years than G-AAXG.

The New Zealand Tiger Club meeting at Waipukurau, Hawke's Bay, in February 1989, was characterised by some rather unseasonal cold, wet, windy weather. Here Gerald Grocott's DH60M(R) ZK-AEJ, flown by Bill Shaw, banks steeply away from the camera amidst some of the showers. The aircraft normally resides at Bridge Pa airfield, Hastings, and was photographed on 6 February 1989.

DH60G III MOTH MAJOR

Further development of the Gipsy I engine led to the Gipsy II of 120 hp. Development of this engine led to the inverted running Gipsy III of the same power. On fitting this engine to the wooden DH60 airframe an immediate improvement was noted in the forward visibility along with a much smoother line as a result of better cowling arrangements. This aircraft was put into small scale production as a club aircraft and was named the DH60G III. Fifty seven aircraft were built in the c/n series 5000–5056. This includes the prototype G-ABUI which flew in March 1932.

Continued refinement of the Gipsy III led to the Gipsy Major of 130 hp. When this engine was fitted to the DH60G III airframe G-ACNP (c/n 5057) the aircraft became known as the DH60G III Moth Major — a strange blend of titles. Ninety six aircraft were built with the Gipsy Major engine at Stag Lane with c/ns from 5057–5152. One other, G-ADIO c/n 2263, was built by apprentices at the DH Technical School in 1935.

DH60G III HB-UPE c/n 5078
Left: At the time of writing HB-UPE is the only airworthy DH60G III Moth Major in the world. Built in 1934 the aircraft was originally registered CH-348, under the old Swiss registration system, and delivered to the Basel Aero Club. It was later sold to Werner Schetty. In 1955 the aircraft was sold to the Aero Club de Lausanne and then, in 1973, it passed on to the Groupement Avion Historique, a Lausanne-based group formed specifically to stop the aircraft from being exported. In 1979 it underwent a complete rebuild to its current standard. This photograph was taken over Lac Lemain on 2 October 1988.

DH80A PUSS MOTH

Although resembling the DH80A in outline the prototype DH80 (or Moth III, as it was at first known) was a somewhat different machine to the production aircraft which followed it. The main difference lay in the fuselage, the prototype having conventional wooden longeron, former and stringer construction with plywood covering. This single prototype (c/n 396) had an inverted Gipsy III engine of 120hp which was fully enclosed. First flight took place, with Class 'B' marks E1, at Stag Lane on 9 September 1929. The aircraft was later registered G-AAHZ.

Performance was actually better than predicted by 7mph. This was considered to be due to the high mounted wing giving less than expected interference drag.

Experience with the steel tube construction of the DH60M led to a decision that the production DH80s would have this form of construction for the fuselage. Seating for one pilot and one passenger was provided in a fully enclosed cabin. A third passenger could be carried if required.

The production aircraft was known as the DH80A and, for a time, continued to be referred to as the Moth III but was soon dubbed the 'Puss Moth' and was allotted c/ns in the range 2001–2260. Aircraft built in Canada had c/ns from DHC 201–DHC 225.

The two-spar wooden wings could be folded for storage and were braced by V-struts.

The undercarriage was of the divided, tailwheel type with the main gear strut braced to the top fuselage longeron. Because of the aircraft's clean design, and flat gliding angle, these struts could be rotated through 90 degrees to increase drag and shorten the landing run.

The early days of the Puss Moth saw a few accidents to the type which all seemed to have a common cause — structural failure of the wing. It was discovered that a combination of high speed and turbulence precipitated the failures. Modifications were carried out and the type subsequently made many record-breaking flights in the hands of people such as Amy Johnson and Jim Mollison.

DH80A G-AEOA c/n 2184

Left: This immaculate Puss Moth is one of only three flyable machines in the world. 'EOA was once owned by erstwhile DH collector Tony Haig-Thomas but is now in the care of Paul and Andrew Wood and based at Old Warden. Impressed into RAF service as ES921 it subsequently became YU-PAX and then UN-PAX before taking up its previous marks as G-AEOA on its return to the UK.

Michael Vaisey flew the aircraft for this photo session over the Cambridge countryside, at harvest time, en route from Audley End to Old Warden and the start of the 'Famous Grouse' Moth Club rally on 18 August 1989.

DH80A G-ABLS c/n 2164

Above: Restored to flying condition by Cliff Lovell, Puss Moth G-ABLS has been owned by Roger Bailey for some years. Now based at Hereford it was photographed during 1977.

DH80A G-AAZP c/n 2047

Right: Justly famous for their record-breaking long distance flights, the story of the Puss Moth did not end in the thirties. This particular example was flown by its owner, Tim Williams, and friend Henry Labouchere from Mildenhall to Melbourne to commemorate the 50th anniversary of the MacRobertson Air Race in 1984. Even in those years this was an arduous journey, expecially for such an elderly lady.

A somewhat less onerous task was the photo session on 23 September 1989 with Tim at the controls.

DH82 TIGER MOTH

Arguably the most famous of all de Havilland designs the DH82 Tiger Moth was the result of a continuous line of improvement and modification to the DH60 series of aircraft.

The last of the DH60 line was the DH60T, itself a development of the DH60M. Designed primarily as a full dual control training aircraft, it could also carry various items of operational equipment. The increased weight required that the structure be strengthened to cope with the extra loads. A new wing section was introduced with a modified structure. The exhaust was arranged to point straight downwards from the engine. This allowed doors to be fitted to both sides of both cockpits. The doors were enlarged to allow greater freedom of entry and exit.

One of the major problems of the earlier DH60 variants was the difficulty of getting into and out of the front cockpit due to the routeing of the rear flying wires from the top of the rear interplane strut to the rear lower wing root. The rear cabane strut also got in the way. With the DH60T it was a requirement that the front seat occupant could escape quickly, in an emergency, with a parachute. The rear flying wire was rerouted but the cabane strut was still in place. The problem was only partially solved and only a small number were built.

The requirement still remained for a two seat trainer with easy egress from the front seat in an emergency so de Havilland took the DH60T and tried ways of doing away with the offending cabane strut. The solution was to move the entire top wing centre section forwards. This left the front seat even easier to get into and out of but it meant that the centre of pressure was going to be in the wrong place if the wings were put back as before. To bring it back to its rightful place the solution was to add sweepback to the top wing.

Experience of the benefits of using the Gipsy III engine in the DH60G III and in the DH80A dictated that this engine be used in the new training aircraft. For a brief period this was known as the DH60T Tiger Moth.

During September 1931 an aircraft was built with increased sweepback and with greater dihedral on the lower wing. With these modifications it was decided to change the type number and the DH82 was born.

What has come to be regarded as the first DH82 was flown at Stag Lane on 26 October 1931 as E-6, later G-ABRC. An initial order for 35 aircraft was placed. These early DH82s could be identified by the fabric-covered rear decking.

Further development of the Gipsy III engine led to the Gipsy Major of 130hp. Adding this engine to the DH82, along with other slight

improvements, produced the DH82A, one of the world's greatest training aircraft.

Initial production took place at Stag Lane until transferred to Hatfield in 1934 and was then transferred again to Cowley, near Oxford, in 1941 to make room for Mosquito production at Hatfield. Further production took place at Toronto, Sydney, Rongotai, New Zealand, Portugal, Norway and Sweden, with the DH82A serving in many of the world's Air Forces, flying schools and clubs. In excess of 8,000 aircraft were produced and it was the mainstay of the Commonwealth Air Training Plan serving with EFTSs in the UK, Rhodesia, South Africa and Canada. With the end of the war many DH82As were surplus to requirements and were stored until they could be sold on to the civil market.

DH82A G-BFHH c/n 85933

Right: Low down over the sea, Peter Harrison poses his Tiger Moth, G-BFHH, in front of Beachy Head lighthouse, Sussex, on 17 October 1989.

Below: During the 1930s the Duchess of Bedford was an avid flier of de Havilland aircraft. Now, in the eighties and leading into the nineties the present Duke and Duchess of Bedford kindly allow the DH Moth Club to use part of their grounds for their annual meeting. The 1988 meet was characterised by cold blustery winds and heavy rain-showers. Caught by the camera are some of the assembled masses of Tigers and other types during a brighter spell.

DH82A G-AOZH/K2572
Above: Flying over the patchwork quilt of the English
countryside is Vic Wheeles' DH82A painted in the yellow
Flying Training colours of the Second World War.

DH82A G-ADXT c/n 3436
Right: Originally registered in December 1935 and then
impressed into RAF service in January 1941 as BB860,
DH82A G-ADXT was rebuilt by John Pothecary using
components from various Tigers. Photographed on 31 August
1981 it is finished in the yellow and silver scheme of the Reid
and Sigrist Flying School. Pilot for the occasion was Bev Pook.

DH82A G-ADXT c/n 3436

Above: During 1988 'DXT was sold to British Airways captain Roger Hanauer to be based at Goodwood, Sussex. At Roger's request the aircraft was repainted in this dark blue and silver scheme. This atmospheric shot was taken near Shoreham, during an air test for the renewal of the aircraft's Permit to Fly, on 5 August 1988.

DH82A G-AOEI c/n 82916

Right: A summer's day with a high sun and a Tiger on a grass airfield. The Cambridge Flying Group's Tiger Moth awaits its next flight.

G-ACDC/G-AOAA/G-AAHY

Above: Framed by DH60M, G-AAHY, are two of the Tiger Club's famous Tiger Moths. The elderly G-ACDC sits alongside the 'Super Tiger' G-AOAA 'The Deacon'. The shot was taken, at Redhill, when 'HY was still in the ownership of Ian White. She is now owned by Michael Vaisey and kept at Old Warden.

G-AOAA was one of four Tigers modified by the Tiger Club, in the days when C. A. Nepean-Bishop was the CFI, for racing. A Gipsy Major 1C of 145hp was fitted and the centre section tank removed. A new fuel tank was placed in the front cockpit which was then faired over. Other aircraft modified were G-APDZ 'The Bishop', G-ANZZ 'The Archbishop', and G-ANMZ 'The Cannon'.

DH82A G-APLU c/n 85094

Left: The Intrepid Flying Group's recently rebuilt DH82A, G-APLU, was photographed on 18 August 1989, en route from Old Warden to Audley End, in the hands of group member Michael Vaisey. Previous identities were VR-AAY and F-OBKK.

DH82A G-ANLH c/n 86546

Right: Rebuilt by Ron Souch and later purchased by Brian Woodford is Tiger Moth G-ANLH. Previous identities have been variously N3744F, OO-EVO, and PG637. The aircraft is now resident at Chalmington but is seen here with Ron Souch and Richard Riding enjoying a Sunday afternoon ride around Woburn Abbey.

Below: John Pothecary refuelling DH82A G-ADXT at Shoreham, on 5 August 1988.

DH82A G-ACMD c/n 3195

Right: Built in December 1933, c/n 3195 was sold to the Spanish Air Force becoming 33-5. Initially based at Alcala d Henares it was detached, in 1935, to Cabo Juby in Spanish Morocco during the Civil War. After the War it was reserialled 33-104 by the Nationalist Air Force and operated by the Advanced Flying School at San Javier and, subsequently, at Barrajas. After retiring from Air Force service it was allotted the civil registration EC-AGB and flown by the Aero Club of Seville until 1965. After lying dormant it was shipped to California in 1971 as N182DH and then back to the U.K. in 1986. Passing through various hands it was acquired by John Pothecary in 1988 as a restoration project and flew again on 10 August 1991. The period registration G-ACMD was obtained from the CAA. This was originally allotted to an Avro Cadet but was not taken up. 'CMD is pictured over Arundel Castle and Cathedral, Sussex, on 9 September 1991 with John at the controls.

Below: Moths on the grass in the summer. Three DH82As grace the grass at Woburn in August 1989. The farthest is G-APAM which was converted to a Jackaroo and has now been converted back to being a DH82A again.

DH82A ZK-BEF

Opposite page: 'Love is a Tiger for two'. So says the drawing on the fin of Graeme Taylor's Tiger ZK-BEF seen cavorting amongst the clouds on 6 February 1989 during the New Zealand Tiger Club's rally at Waipukurau, Hawkes Bay, North Island.

DH82A G-BLAX/N6848

Right: Air under her wings again, G-BLAX climbs away from Gransden during the de Havilland Moth Club meet in August 1975.

DH82A ZK-ALK

Below: Richard and Kathy Broussard of Louisiana flying John Crosbie's Tiger ZK-ALK over some typical North Island terrain heading south towards Gisborne, in the north east of the island, on 6 February 1989.

DH82A G-ANEZ c/n 84218

Right: In military service as T7849 this DH82A was registered as G-ANEZ on 20 October 1953. Owned by Chris Bland and Terry Warren it has been based at Sandown on the Isle of Wight since 1964. Chris was flying the aircraft for this photograph approaching The Needles at the western end of the island on 29 October 1988.

DH82A G-ANRM c/n 85861

Overleaf: In RAF service as DF112 this aircraft was registered as G-ANRM on 8 June 1954 and is seen here, shortly after a rebuild, being flown by Paul Groves, over Woburn Abbey on 15 August 1987.

DH82A G-ACDC c/n 3177

Right: Almost the oldest flyable Tiger Moth in the world 'CDC resides at the Redhill home of the Tiger Club where Club members can take her out for an hour's gentle aerobatics. She is seen here over the Surrey countryside on 23 September 1987.

DH82A G-ALRI/T5672 c/n 83350

Below: Stick well forward, get the tail up early in the take off run, judicious use of the rudder. All are required to help prevent the swing on take off in which the combined gyroscopic and torque forces conspire to catch the unwary. Here G-ALRI/T5672 commences its take off run at owner Brian Woodford's strip at Chalmington Manor in the late summer of 1988.

DH82B Queen Bee G-BLUZ/LF858

Right: At first sight the DH82B looks like a standard DH82A Tiger Moth but closer inspection reveals the wooden fuselage of a Moth Major with Tiger Moth wings and tail surfaces. The aircraft was a hybrid intended for cheap production as a gunnery target. When operational they were fitted with floats and launched from catapults. A conventional wheeled undercarriage was fitted for ferrying between land bases.

First flight of the DH82B took place at Hatfield on 5 January 1935, with a test pilot at the controls. It was normally flown from the front seat as the rear cockpit was given to the rather cumbersome radio equipment. Three hundred and eighty aircraft were produced at Hatfield and Glasgow.

Considering their intended fate a great many DH82Bs survived the war and were put into store to be later obtained by Rollasons who stripped them of all the usable Tiger Moth parts and burnt the fuselages.

Only two examples are now known to exist — one in a museum in Minneapolis and the one illustrated which is the only airworthy example in the world, G-BLUZ/LF858. This is a Glasgow-built example and was stored at Old Warden for many years until it was restored to flying condition by Barry Bayes who is seen here at the controls on 15 August 1987.

Thruxton Jackaroo C-FPHZ

Left: Take a standard DH82A, add a new centre section to the fuselage, with a wider track undercarriage and a Gipsy Major 10 of 145 hp and the result is a faster aeroplane with four seats — the Thruxton Jackaroo. A number of DH82As were converted by Jackaroo Aircraft Ltd. at Thruxton Airfield, Hampshire, between 1957 and 1959.

Jackaroo C-FPHZ started life as DH82A N6924, c/n 82168, on the Hatfield production line in 1939. Taken on charge by 6 MU at Brize Norton on 3 July 1939, it was allotted to 22 EFTS at Cambridge on 15 September 1939. With the end of the war the aircraft was stored until bought by the Wiltshire School of Flying, as G-APHZ, on 3 April 1951. In 1958 it was one of the airframes converted to Jackaroo configuration. In this guise it passed through many hands until bought by B. H. Witty on 19 August 1970 and taken to Canada where it became CF-QOT. It was later sold to Glen Norman who twice flew it across Canada and then sold it to Gert Frank in the USA.

In 1978 the aircraft was bought by its present owners, Tom Dietrich and Frank D. Evans, who had it registered C-FPHZ. After a five year restoration she was Antique Custom Champion at Oshkosh in 1983 and has taken various awards at other events since.

In all nineteen Jackaroos were built, including one by Rollason Aircraft Ltd. 'PHZ is one of a tiny handful remaining in the world and is seen here flying near her base at Guelph, Ontario with Charlie Miller at the controls on 15 May 1989.

DH82C CF-GTU/4319

Above: With the outbreak of war in 1939, plans were made to increase manufacture of the DH82A Tiger Moth in Canada to provide training aircraft for the flying training schemes being devised in that country to ensure an adequate supply of pilots for the rapidly expanding RAF. Some thirty DH82A (Canada) aircraft were manufactured in 1938–39 but in excess of 1500 DH82Cs were completed prior to 1942.

The DH82C was designed to be more suitable for Canadian conditions, the most obvious difference being the sliding cockpit canopy. Not so obvious was a new cowling hinged on the centre line, for easier access to the engine, wheel brakes, metal interplane struts and a tailwheel. The undercarriage was raked forward to prevent nosing over if the brakes were applied too harshly. Along with the new canopy came a redesign of the cockpit layout and lower sills.

With the loss of some ships to U-boats in the North Atlantic there was a shortage of Gipsy Major engines and an American engine, the Menasco Pirate D-4 of 120 hp was substituted on some DH82Cs. This engine no longer flies on this type.

CF-GTU (RCAF serial 4319) was in service between 1940 and 1951 serving, initially, with No.8 and then No.19 EFTS at Boundary Bay, British Columbia then later at Trenton. A spell with No.12 EFTS followed at Goderich, Ontario. On retiral from the RCAF she continued to train civilian pilots at Goderich and then Sarnia. Glider towing and a time on floats followed.

After being bought by Toronto Airways 'GTU was restored to her original RCAF marks between 1965–67 and is today kept at Buttonville Airport, Ontario.

The photograph here was taken during a sortie on 17 May 1989 with Watt Martin at the controls near Milton, Ontario.

DH83 FOX MOTH

The DH83 Fox Moth was one of those lovely British improvisations of a proven design that was a great success. Designer Arthur Hagg had a problem — how to get himself and his family to the coast quickly and easily to enjoy the yachting which was his other love. The answer was to take the wings, tail unit and engine from a Tiger Moth and wed them to a new fuselage. The fuselage could accommodate a pilot and four passengers although three were preferred if any great range was required. The engine was to be a Gipsy III.

The new fuselage was of standard de Havilland spruce and plywood design and passengers could enter via doors on either side of the fully enclosed cabin. The pilot, in early production machines, sat in an open cockpit behind the wings. On later machines an enclosed sliding canopy was fitted. The lower wing roots were modified to allow the wings to fold although this feature was deleted from the post-war Canadian production aircraft. Unlike the DH82A the wing struts on all but the prototype, G-ABUO, were of steel tube. This prototype first flew at Stag Lane on 29 January 1932 and shortly afterwards was shipped to Canada for trials on both floats and skis. Registered CF-API it flew until 1950.

Many operators used Fox Moths as mini airliners including Edward Hillman of Hillman Airways. Altogether 98 Fox Moths were built in the UK with another two being built in Australia. As was becoming usual for DH types many Foxes were sold around the world. Canada proved to be a particularly good market with its load carrying ability being useful in the Canadian Bush.

In 1946 de Havilland (Canada) was trying to recover from the sudden cancellation of aircraft orders after the Allies victories in Europe and the Far East. There was still a demand from the Canadian Bush fliers for a good aeroplane with a good lifting capability so it was decided to put the DH83 back into production using surplus DH82C parts until a more modern type could be designed and put into production. The 'new' aircraft was to be designated DH83C and was powered by a Gipsy Major 1C of 145 hp, had a strengthened floor and a new, wider door on the port side to cope with bulky loads. Brakes and a DH82C type tailwheel were fitted and all aircraft had a redesigned sliding canopy.

Fifty three DH83Cs were produced in the c/n range FM-1 to FM-54 (FM-53 was not completed).

DH83 G-ACEJ c/n 4069
Left: Operated by Giro Aviation for some thirty years Fox Moth G-ACEJ was sold to the Tiger Club in 1966 before passing on to collector Tony Haig-Thomas. Pictured here at Cranfield in 1973 it was destroyed at Old Warden when another aircraft crashed into it on take off and it burst into flames on 17 July 1982. Like the proverbial phoenix from the ashes it is being rebuilt by Ben Cooper at Newbury.

DH83C CF-DJB c/n FM28

Below: One of the bush pilots struggling to make a living in Canada after the war was a young man named Maxwell Ward. Max grew up in Edmonton, Alberta and joined the RCAF, learning to fly in 1941. On discharge from the Air Force he made plans to start operating in the Yellowknife area — he was only lacking an aeroplane.

In August 1946 Max arrived at Downsview, Toronto, with the intention of buying a Fox Moth. Although he did not have enough capital to buy the aircraft outright a deal was struck and the Polaris Charter Company began operating with DH83C CF-DJC c/n FM29. From that lowly beginning the charter airline Wardair was built.

That original Fox Moth is now no more and its registration is now worn by one of Wardair's Boeing 747s. Max, remembering his beginnings, wanted to have another Fox Moth to be painted exactly as his first. In January 1973 he bought DH83C CF-DJB c/n FM28 from its owner Jack Edwards of Kenora, Ontario and it was painted to represent CF-DJC. At this time, though, it was not fully representative of 'DJC as the Canadian authorities demanded it have the new style registration of C-FDJB. It just did not look right.

On 5 September 1976 the aircraft stalled into Lake Ontario and suffered considerable damage. A rebuild was possible but a new fuselage had to be made. On completion the Canadian authorities relented and allowed the 'proper' marks to be carried. Kept at Toronto International Airport the aircraft flew only rarely to go to Watt Martin's strip at Milton for its annual maintenance and for a few weeks to appear in a film for which it was fitted with floats.

On 15 May 1989 CF-DJB was flown to Ottawa to be placed into the Canadian Transport Museum. Immediately before that flight Max Ward allowed me to take the last air to air shots of 'DJB. Pilot for the occasion was former de Havilland (Canada) test pilot George Neal with Watt Martin as the camera plane pilot.

DH83 G-ADHA c/n 4097

Right: The last British-built Fox Moth, 'DHA was originally registered in New Zealand as ZK-ADI in December 1934. Owned by one Bert Mercer it provided transport for mail, freight and passengers from Hokitika to some of the more remote areas of New Zealand.

During April 1943 it was impressed into RNZAF service as NZ566 and was to remain as such until July 1948 when it was re-registered as ZK-ASP with the National Airways Corporation. It was replaced by a Dominie in 1954 and passed into private ownership for the next 20 years. In 1974 'ASP was taken to the USA where it was damaged. Following this accident it was sold to a new owner in New York state and registered N83DH.

Some years later, after very little flying, N83DH was bought by Brian Woodford for his collection at Chalmington, Dorset. Restored by Ron Souch and his team the aircraft is now painted in the royal navy blue, plum and chrome colours of the Prince of Wales' aircraft, G-ACDD, as it appeared in the 1930s.

Here, Ron Souch is flying the aircraft on 20 August 1986.

DH83C G-AOJH c/n FM42

Below: A Canadian-built machine, G-AOJH was originally
sold in Pakistan as AP-ABO and remained there until it was
ferried back to the UK, arriving at Southend on 24 September
1955. Purchased by John Lewery it was used for joy-riding at
various locations around the coast including Bournemouth,
Blackpool, Southport and, latterly, at Shoreham, west of
Brighton. This photograph was taken during a test flight after
C of A renewal on 27 April 1983, with John Pothecary at the
controls.

DH84 DRAGON

After his success operating the DH83 Fox Moth, Edward Hillman, of Hillman Airways, approached the de Havilland Aircraft Company to enquire about the possibility of constructing a twin-engined successor to that aircraft with the same, or better, operating economics, with which to operate his services to the Continent. He was shown Arthur E. Hagg's drawings of a twin-engined, two bay, biplane powered by Gipsy Major 1 engines which had been designed to an Iraqi Air Force requirement. He was sufficiently impressed to order four machines 'off the drawing board' at a cost of £2,795 each.

Thus was born the DH84 Dragon. It could, initially, seat six passengers with a single pilot. Later the seating was raised to eight with a luggage limit of 45 lbs per passenger. Construction was typical for de Havilland using spruce and plywood with fabric-covered wings and tailplane.

The fuselage was 34 ft 6 ins long, covered with plywood and extensively glazed, as was the cockpit, which gave the pilot an extremely good view over the short nose, and to the sides, as he was well in front of the engines which could be easily seen from the 'office'. Access to the cockpit was gained via the passenger cabin along the single aisle and through a door in the front bulkhead.

The engines were neatly cowled Gipsy Major 1s giving 130 hp at 2,350 rpm and 120 hp at 2,100 rpm in the cruise. Each engine had its own 30 gallon fuel tank behind it and was fed by a DHAC fuel pump as the 'head' was insufficient for a gravity feed. Under the fuel tank was a separate two gallon oil tank.

The wingspan was 47 ft 4 ins, the spars being of spindled I-section with wooden ribs. All four wings had differential ailerons fitted. The wings were made to fold just outboard of the engines. The undercarriage was of the divided semi-cantilever type with a single wheel and a 12 ft track.

The prototype DH84 flew, at Stag Lane, with the manufacturer's Class 'B' registration E9, on 24 November 1932 with Hubert Broad at the controls. In December of that year it was delivered to Maylands aerodrome, Romford, Essex, complete with its new registration of G-ACAN and painted in the blue, white and silver colours of Hillman Airways. Operating economics were soon found to be even better than those of the Fox Moth. A production line was set up and, eventually, 115 aircraft were sold in various parts of the world. C/ns 6000–6061 were Dragons Mk1 and 6062–6114 were Dragons Mk2 which differed mainly in having separate, framed cabin windows and a faired undercarriage. A production line was also set up at Bankstown, Sydney, Australia, generating a further 87 aircraft (c/ns 2001–2087) to approximately the Mk1 standard.

DH84 Dragon 2 EI-ABI, c/n 6105

Right: The original EI-ABI was actually a different machine to the one illustrated here. Registered G-ACPY (c/n 6076) it was sold to Olley Air Services Ltd. The first C of A was issued on 10 May 1934. In February 1935 'CPY was sold to Blackpool and West Coast Air Services. May 27 1936 saw 'CPY as the sole aircraft in the fleet of the newly formed Aer Lingus when it operated the airline's first service from Baldonnel to Bristol. After the purchase of the airline's second aircraft, a DH86A, the Dragon named 'Iolar' (Eagle), served the Baldonnel–Liverpool route with occasional forays to the Isle of Man.

Iolar was restored to the British register, as G-ACPY, on 1 March 1938, to be operated again by Olley Air Services. It was lost on 3 June 1941, whilst being operated by Great Western and Southern Airlines, on a service from the Scilly Isles to Land's End. It is believed to have been shot down by a Ju88 which was known to have been in the area at the time.

The aircraft illustrated here started life as G-AECZ (c/n 6105) with Air Cruises Ltd on 18 April 1936. As with many other civil aircraft at the time it was impressed into service with 24 Squadron RAF on 11 October 1939, becoming AV982.

After the end of the war it returned to civilian use with Air Taxis of Croydon on 18 June 1946 and then, in 1948, it was purchased by the Wiltshire School of Flying at Thruxton.

In 1950 'ECZ found its final home in Ireland where it was sold to Weston Ltd and registered EI-AFK. It flew on charter and pleasure flights for nine years until its wings were folded in 1959 for, seemingly, the last time.

Aer Lingus became interested in the aircraft and, in 1967, it was bought and repainted in the colours of the original Dragon EI-ABI 'Iolar'. It remained at Colinstown, hangared, for a further four years until, on 6 March 1971 it was taken out to the taxiway at Dublin to escort the airline's first Boeing 747 on its arrival at Dublin. After this brief outing 'ABI was tucked away in the hangar again. May 1976 saw the Dragon being put back in the air again but the 'lift' was provided by steel cables as the aircraft was suspended from the ceiling of Dublin's terminal building as part of an aeronautical exhibition.

With the 50th anniversary of Aer Lingus' birth imminent John Molloy, of the Airline's quality assurance department suggested that the aircraft be made airworthy again. Aer Lingus agreed to finance the restoration work and, in August 1985, the aircraft was officially re-registered EI-ABI. The first post-restoration flight took place on 10 April 1986.

On 25 July EI-ABI stopped at Shoreham during its journey to Redhill from Dublin for an air to air photo sortie. Pilot for the occasion was Aer Lingus captain Paul Van Lonkhuyzen.

DH84 Dragon 2 N34DH c/n 6096

Left and above: N34DH is a Hatfield-built Dragon. Its first C of A was issued on 18 May 1935 and the aircraft was delivered to its first owner, Railway Air Services, as G-ADDI.

On 22 September 1939 the aircraft was impressed into RAF service with 24 Squadron at Hendon. No record of any military serial appears to exist. 'DDI was used to ferry personnel and supplies to the Continent until June 1940 when it was transferred to the Associated Airways Joint Committee until sold, in 1943 to Vickers Armstrong as a Company transport.

After the war the aircraft was sold to Mr G. A. Phelps on 23 May 1946. On 22 August 1947 'DDI was bought by Air Charter Ltd. The pleasure flying career of 'DDI started in March 1951 when the aircraft was flown to Squires Gate, Blackpool, where it joined Air Navigation and Trading. In November 1962 the aircraft was taken over by Aero Enterprises (JHS) Ltd and operated by Chrisair in whose colours it is still painted and in which it is best remembered.

'DDI continued pleasure flying and charter work until May 1968 when it was withdrawn from use. It remained stored at Sywell until purchased for the Perlitch Transport Museum, Morgan Hill, California. On 21 February 1971 it was flown, as N34DH, to Rotterdam for shipment to the USA.

Mike Kimbrell, a Boeing 727 captain with Delta Airlines, found, and bought the aircraft in April 1981 and flew it along the Pacific coast to his strip outside his farm home some 80 miles south of Seattle, Washington. Here 'DDI flies regularly — an established de Havilland presence in the Boeing heartland.

Photograph is of Mike Kimbrell flying N34DH over the pine clad hills of Washington State near Oakville during a sortie on 2 September 1988.

Above: DH84 Dragon EI-ABI at Redhill.

DH85 LEOPARD MOTH

Although similar in appearance to the DH80A Puss Moth the DH85 Leopard Moth was rather different in many areas. Whereas the DH80A was essentially a two seat aircraft with provision for a third occupant the DH85 was designed from the start to accommodate three people, including the pilot. It had been noted that the current vogue of steel tube construction was producing aircraft which were noticeably heavier than their wooden equivalents, and they were also more expensive to manufacture, so the DH85s fuselage reverted to the old, tried and tested de Havilland wooden stringer, former and plywood covered design.

Construction methods of the Puss and Leopard's wings were almost identical but the shape differed considerably in planform, the Leopard having a swept leading edge. Bracing was in the form of two V-struts and the wings could fold for hangarage.

The undercarriage of the Puss Moth had a telescopic shock strut attached to the upper fuselage by the forward wing attachment but, in the DH85, this was moved to a point by the engine bulkhead. Like the DH80A, and the later DH87, the fairing on this strut could be rotated through 90 degrees to act as an airbrake and to steepen the glide for landing.

Fuel tanks in the wings contained 35 gallons to feed the Gipsy Major which gave a cruise speed of 120 mph and a maximum speed of 142 mph. Still air range was a respectable 715 miles.

The first DH85 was registered E-1 and, later, G-ACHD and was flown by Geoffrey de Havilland on 27 May 1933. On 13 July he took it to victory in the King's Cup Air Race at 139.5 mph. Not bad for a new type!

Later in its career this aircraft was fitted with a Gipsy Six (R) engine of 230 hp and was used to test the Hamilton and the Ratier variable pitch propellers destined for the DH88 Comet Racers and, as such, was known as the DH85A.

A total of 132 Leopard Moths were built in the c/n block 7000.

DH85 G-ACUS c/n 7082
Overleaf: The DH85 Leopard Moth is now a very rare bird indeed. Only four examples are known to be airworthy at the time of writing. This example, G-ACUS, is owned by Torquil Norman and based near Swindon. The aircraft spent some time in Switzerland as HB-OXA and, on return to the UK, was rebuilt using parts from another Leopard Moth, HB-OXO.

Photographed high over the Wiltshire countryside on 23 September 1989, 'CUS was being flown for the occasion by Tim Williams, owner of DH80A Puss Moth G-AAZP.

DH87 HORNET MOTH

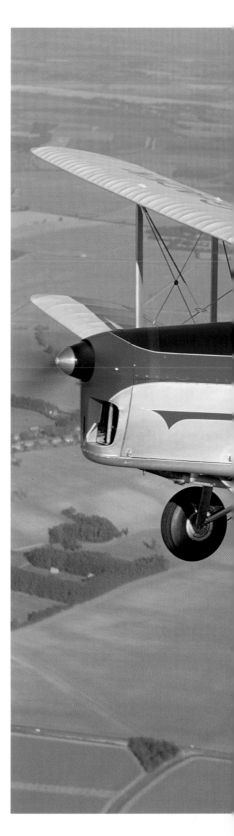

By 1933 the creature comforts of an enclosed cabin and cockpit heating were being demanded by buyers of light aircraft. The DH80A Puss Moth and the DH85 Leopard Moth had paved the way for de Havilland in this respect but there was now a perceived need for a Gipsy Moth replacement for club, instruction and general touring use. With this in mind a cabin biplane arrangement was set down on paper. An experiment in side-by-side seating was thought a good idea to test the merits of this layout for training and so the DH87 Hornet Moth was born.

Flown by Geoffrey de Havilland, the first DH87 took to the air at Hatfield on 9 May 1934, as E-6 (c/n 1997). Shortly afterwards it was registered G-ACTA and flown in the King's Cup Air Race on 13 July but was, unfortunately, eliminated in the heats.

The first DH87 had various snags but these were mostly soon cured. The production aircraft had a completely different wing design, being of greater span and more sharply tapered than the prototypes rounded wingtip design. This new version was dubbed the DH87A.

Experience in service rapidly showed that this wing design, although good in the cruise, gave problems in handling at low speeds as it was inclined to drop a wing near the stall due to the sharp taper and the pointed wingtips. A third new wing was designed with only slight taper and squared tips and this was tested on the third DH87 built, G-ADIS. Results were much more satisfactory and this wing was adopted as the standard on the '1936 Hornet', officially known as the DH87B. The new wing was offered as a retrofit to owners of existing DH87As.

Construction of the DH87B was of mixed steel tube and wood for the fuselage and wood for the wings and tail surfaces. Power was provided by a Gipsy Major of 130 hp giving a speed of 105 mph. The DH87A, having less induced drag, had a higher speed of 111 mph.

Like the Puss and Leopard Moths, the Hornet Moth had a rather flat glide and so the same solution was applied in the form of fairings on the undercarriage legs which could be rotated through 90 degrees to act as airbrakes to slow the aircraft quickly and steepen the glide. General handling of the DH87B was good with each pilot having a control column. This column was actually mounted centrally, between the occupants and was split into a V-shape part way up thus saving on the weight and complexity of two separate sets of controls. A 36 gallon fuel tank behind the cockpit gave a range of 620 miles in the DH87B, with plenty of spare room for luggage when touring.

In total 165 Hornet Moths were built at Hatfield in the c/n block 8000–8163, plus the prototype (1997).

DH87B G-ADKK c/n 8033

Above: This shot of DH87B G-ADKK was taken at the Moth Club meeting at Gransden Lodge, England, during the long hot summer of 1976 with its owner Cliff Anniss at the controls. At the time Cliff had just completed a major refurbishment of 'DKK which was kept at Boston, Lincolnshire.

This aircraft was first registered on 9 November 1935, and had been impressed into RAF service as W5749.

DH87B G-ADKK

Overleaf: Twelve years after the first photo sortie the author finds himself alongside 'DKK again on 30 September 1988. The aircraft has a new owner in Richard Anniss (no relation to Cliff) and C. P. B. Horsley and is kept on a farm strip at Slinfold near Horsham, Surrey.

DH87B C-FEEJ c/n 8092

Left: Built at Hatfield in 1936 this aircraft was first registered in the UK as G-AEET. With the coming of war 'ET was impressed into RAF service as X9319 and delivered to RAF Mildenhall as a communications aircraft. Shortly afterwards she was based at Honington and then returned to Mildenhall. These bases were only temporary, however, and 'ET was to spend the rest of her brief service career with 3 Group at Newmarket until struck off charge in November 1941. Restored to the civil register in 1942 she was used by de Havillands as a communications aircraft.

From April 1948 'ET was owned, variously, by the Hornet Private Flying Club, Luton; Flt Lt Denis Hittington at RAF West Raynham; P. I. S. Boardman of Yarmouth and Dr R. G. Woodsend of Kings Lynn, Norfolk.

'ETs last flight in the UK was on 5 March 1969 after which she was crated and shipped to Downsview, Ontario, in the new ownership of de Havilland (Canada) test pilot George Neal and registered C-FEEJ. Between 1972–82 'EEJ underwent a complete airframe overhaul and has now flown in excess of 3,100 hours.

The photograph here was taken near Watt Martin's strip at Milton, Ontario, on 18 May 1989, with George at the controls.

DH87B G-AESE c/n 8108

Below: Owned by Geoff Green, 'ESE was first registered on 13 January 1937. Impressed into RAF service it became W5775. Now named 'Sheena', after his wife, Geoff flew the aircraft for the camera on 18 August 1989 near Old Warden.

DH87B G-ADLY/G-AESE

Overleaf: With Colin Dodds flying Victor Gauntlett's G-ADLY, Geoff Green formates his own Hornet, G-AESE 'Sheena' near Old Warden on 18 August 1989, prior to the start of the 'Famous Grouse' Moth rally.

DH88 COMET

The 1920s and 30s were the heydays of air racing. Various entrepreneurs proposed and financed many important air races and pilots winning them were feted as heroes. Industry could see, and took advantage of, the many lessons in aeronautical development to be learnt from these races.

One of the more important races of the time was that from England to Australia proposed by Sir MacPherson Robertson in March 1933. This was to celebrate the founding of the State of Victoria and was to be flown from Mildenhall, Suffolk, England to Melbourne.

To de Havillands the problem was a simple one. It was inconceivable that a foreign aircraft, or crew, should be allowed to win such a prestigious race commencing in England and culminating in part of the Empire. There were no suitable British aircraft available with the required speed and range so the directors of de Havilland decided that they should go ahead and design, and build, an aircraft with the specific intention of winning that race even if it meant a financial loss to the company. The experience and publicity which would ensue would be their reward.

Much publicity was given to de Havillands' offer to build three aircraft. They were to be capable of cruising at more than 200 mph and would be sold for the nominal sum of £5,000 each. Orders had to be received before February 1934 so as to ensure the timely laying down and completion of the airframes for the start of the race at dawn on 20 October 1934.

Three aircraft were ordered off the drawing board by Jim and Amy Mollison, Bernard Rubin and A. O. Edwards, managing director of the Grosvenor House Hotel.

The first DH88 Comet flew at Hatfield, with Class B marks E-1, on 8 September 1934 with Hubert Broad at the controls. This aircraft later became the Mollisons' G-ACSP 'Black Magic'.

The DH88 was a twin-engined low wing cantilever monoplane, the wing being built in one piece, with a retractable undercarriage with tailskid. The wing was built around three wooden box spars with built up ribs and stringers and a covering of laminated plywood strips running diagonally, the whole being covered with doped fabric. Split flaps covered the entire trailing edge from aileron to aileron and also the fuselage section. The ailerons had internal mass balancing.

The undercarriage was manually retracted upwards and rearwards

Left: Breaking hard left 'CSS shows the camera its beautifully tapered elliptical wing designed to give a very low induced drag to achieve high speed on a comparatively low power. Unlike the original aircraft, which was powered by two specially modified Gipsy Six 'R' engines with Ratier two position propellers, the aircraft now has two Gipsy Six engines with de Havilland VP props.

into the engine nacelles, the door being fixed to the undercarriage leg. Each nacelle housed a Gipsy Six 'R' engine of 230hp. It was intended that Hamilton Standard variable pitch propellers would be used but, in the event, French Ratier two position props had to be used instead. These had to be set to 'FINE' pitch on the ground using a bicycle pump and then, in the air, they reset themselves to 'COARSE' by dynamic air pressure at around 150mph. This led to handling problems as, inevitably one would set itself to COARSE before the other. Once in COARSE pitch in the air the props could not be reset to FINE until back on the ground. This made the aircraft interesting to handle on the approach to land. Overshoots were not much fun from low level.

The Gipsy Six 'R' engines were modified Gipsy Sixes with new cylinder heads, valve rocker gear and pistons. The overall height of the engine was reduced by two inches and compression ratio was increased from 5.25 to 6.5. Power was increased from 200hp to 230hp. It was estimated that 6hp of this was from the ram air effect increasing the 'boost' at cruising speed. This power was achieved at 2,400rpm.

The fuselage was also a wooden structure built around four longerons with bulkheads. A wooden skin covered the whole. In highly stressed areas the skin was laminated in a similar fashion to the wing skins. The crew was housed well back in the fuselage, in tandem. Both were provided with flying controls to help overcome the fatigue of long distance flying. (The leg from London to Baghdad was over 2,500 miles.)

Because the wing was so thin (11 inches at its deepest point) all the fuel had to be carried in three tanks in the fuselage. These tanks, of 128 gallons and 110 gallons in front of the pilots and 20 gallons behind the pilots gave the aircraft a range of 2,925 miles.

Wingspan was 44 feet, length was 29 feet. Maximum speed was 237mph and long range cruise was 220mph.

Dawn on 20 October 1934 saw the three DH88s at the start line, at Mildenhall. Even for de Havillands this was a quite remarkable achievement.

G-ACSP (c/n 1994) was the Mollisons' mount finished in black and gold and named 'Black Magic' with the race number 63. Bernard Rubin's machine was G-ACSR (c/n 1995) and was painted green but unnamed. It was crewed by Owen Cathcart-Jones and Ken Waller and had the race number 19. Bernard Rubin was unable to fly himself due to illness. The third aircraft was the scarlet and white G-ACSS 'Grosvenor House' flown by C. W. A. Scott and Tom Campbell Black on behalf of A. O. Edwards. Race number was 34.

The race was an eventful one for the DH88s. 'CSP had to retire at Allahabad with damaged engines. 'CSR had to make a forced landing at Dizful, Persia after losing their way but returned to the race to come fourth with a time of 108 hours 13 minutes 30 seconds. On arrival they picked up newsreels and photographs of the event and returned them to England establishing an out and return record of 13 days 6 hours and 43 minutes after leaving Mildenhall.

G-ACSS, as everyone now knows, won the race to Melbourne in a time of 70 hours 54 minutes 18 seconds, beating the KLM Douglas DC2 flown by K. D. Parmentier.

After the race the French government bought 'CSR which was delivered to Le Bourget on 5 July 1935 as F-ANPY setting a new record for the London–Paris route in the process.

'CSP was sold to Portugal on 25 February 1935, becoming CS-AAJ and was named 'Salazar' under which guise it continued to set further records.

Two further examples were built. F-ANPZ and G-ADEF 'Boomerang' which set further records.

'CSS was shipped back from Melbourne and taken over by the Air Ministry as K5084. After suffering the second of two undercarriage collapses, it was disposed of to F. E. Tasker who had it rebuilt at Gravesend and fitted it with Gipsy Six II engines. It continued to fly and break records until 1938 when it was put under wraps. It was next seen in public in 1951, minus an engine, at the Festival of Britain. It was subsequently put on display at the de Havilland Engine Company's factory at Leavesden.

On 30 October 1965 the aircraft passed into the hands of the Shuttleworth Collection. After a lengthy rebuild, the latter part of which was undertaken by British Aerospace at Hatfield, the aircraft made its second first flight on Sunday 17 May 1987, with George Ellis at the controls.

Only five DH88s were ever built but the contribution they made, during their short career, to aeronautical development, was out of all proportion to their numbers, leading, as they did, to the DH91 Albatross and, of course, to the DH98 Mosquito.

DH88 G-ACSS c/n 1996

Arguably the most famous racing aircraft ever built, the DH88 Comet, G-ACSS, was the third of five aircraft constructed by de Havilland. All were built for racing and high speed record attempts, although the French and Portuguese also used them as high speed mail planes.

'CSS was sponsored in the 1934 MacRobertson Air Race by A. O. Edwards, Managing Director of the 'Grosvenor House' Hotel and won the race in a time of 70 hours 54 minutes with the crew of C. W. A. Scott and Tom Campbell-Black qualifying for both of the main prizes. The rules did not allow for this and so they were awarded the main prize for speed with the handicap prize going to the KLM DC-2 crewed by K. D. Parmentier.

Obtained by the Shuttleworth Collection on 30 October 1965, plans were made to restore the aircraft to airworthiness — a quite massive undertaking. Many firms contributed resources and finances to the project until, after a fourteen

year rebuild, 'CSS took to the air again at Hatfield on 17 May 1987 with BAe test pilot George Elliss at the controls. Its first public appearance was the Shuttleworth Display at Old Warden on 31 May 1987. The aircraft is now kept at Hatfield under the care of British Aerospace.

As a concession to modern hard runways a tailwheel was added rather than the original tailskid. This led to a landing incident and some damage. During the repairs a lockable tailwheel was fitted and the aircraft flew again on 26 August 1988 in time to appear at that year's SBAC display at Farnborough.

Three Shuttleworth display pilots are currently cleared to fly the aircraft, George Elliss, John Lewis and, for this photo sortie, Angus McVitie, who is the Chief Test Pilot at the Cranfield Institute of Technology.

DH88 G-ACSS cockpit

Above: The cockpit of 'CSS is as original as possible but concessions have had to be made to modernity in the form of good NAV/COM equipment.

DH88 G-ACSS c/n 1996

Overleaf: Shot on 27 September 1989 with Angus McVitie at the controls, DH88 G-ACSS shows off its finely sculptured racing lines.

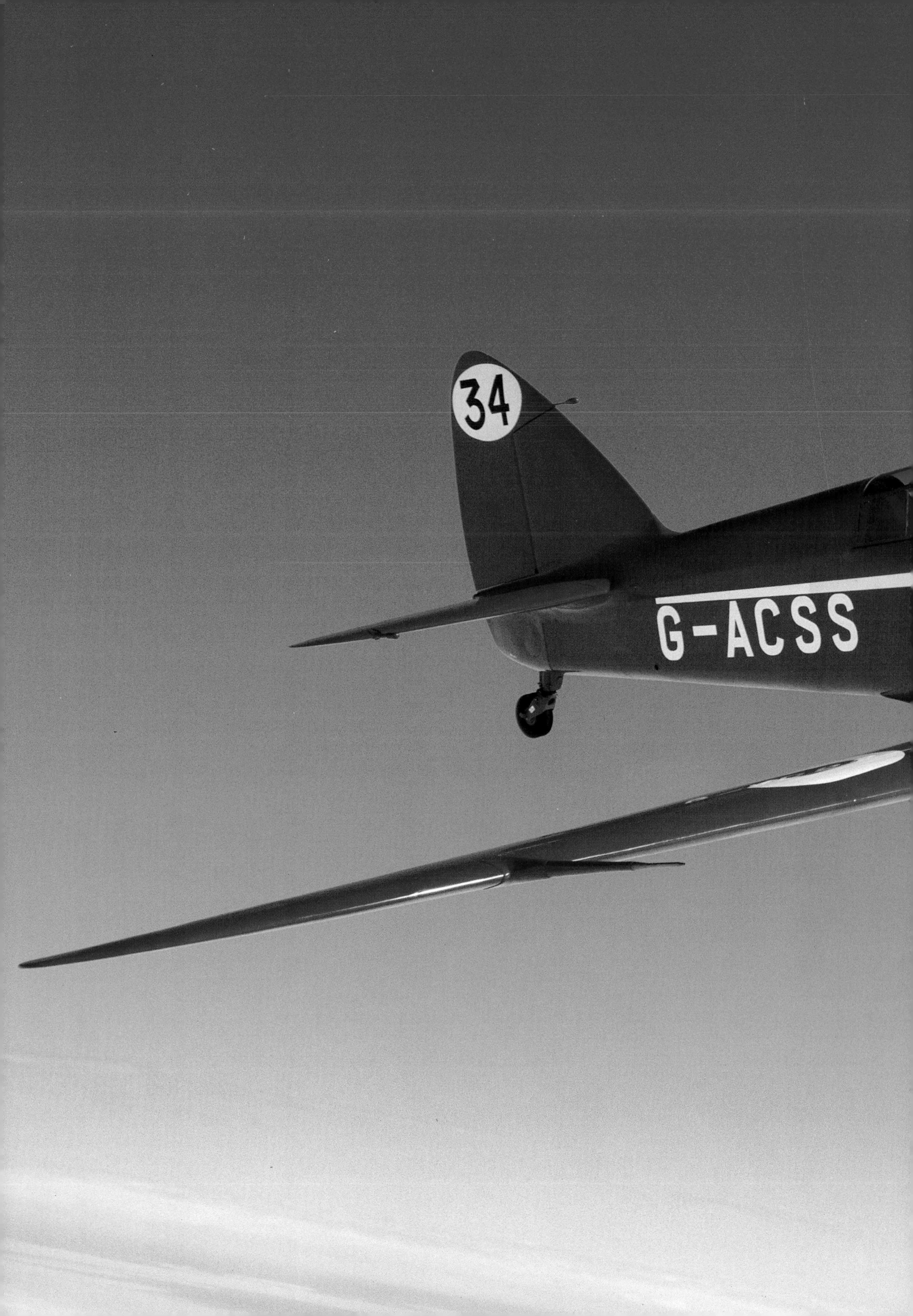
34
G-ACSS

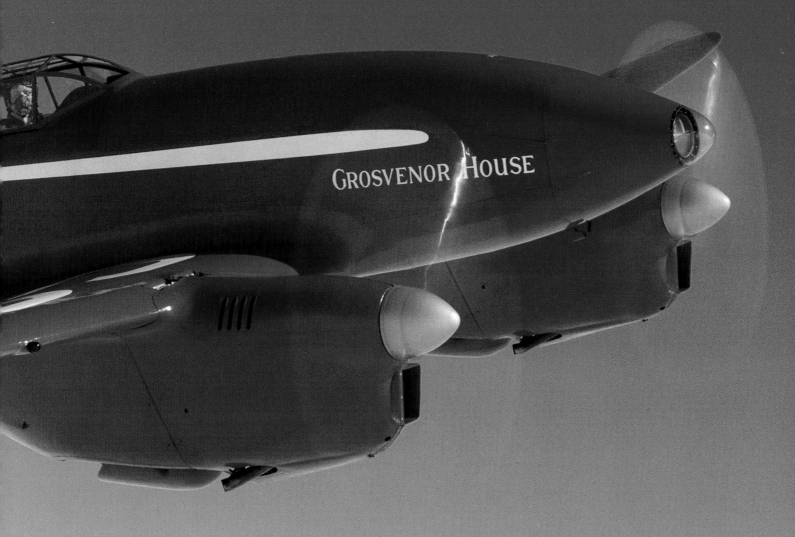

DH89 DRAGON RAPIDE

Looking for a more modern replacement for the DH84 Dragon, de Havilland took the general layout and design of the DH86 'Express' and scaled it down to the size of the DH84. The DH86 (of which not one, alas, exists) was a rather attractive large four-engined biplane airliner using four Gipsy Sixes for power.

Retaining two Gipsy Sixes the resulting aircraft was also a very attractive machine. Given the type number DH89 it was known initially as the Dragon Six. It had beautifully tapered wings, a trousered undercarriage and a minimum of external struts and bracing. Construction was of typical de Havilland type with longerons and spacers of spruce with a plywood covering. Stringers were then added to the outside and the whole was fabric covered, the stringers giving the fuselage a pleasing shape. The nose of the aircraft tapered beautifully to provide a cockpit for a single pilot. The 'quadrant' windows of the cockpit could be opened in flight to provide a clear view in poor weather.

The wing centre section was a massive load-bearing structure terminating just outboard of the engines. The front spar was a steel tube with a wooden rear spar and this section housed the two Gipsy sixes plus the undercarriage, fuel and oil tanks. Loads were transmitted to the rest of the airframe by attachment to the lower fuselage longerons and also by four struts attached to the spars and, thence, to the upper longerons providing a very stable, strong structure.

The upper and lower wings were of all-wood construction, the upper wings being attached directly to the fuselage and the lower wings to the stubs of the centre section, outboard of the engines. The wings were very finely tapered in plan view. Mass balanced ailerons were carried on all four wings, the push rods for the upper ailerons being housed in the streamlined outer strut thus improving appearance and reducing drag.

The first DH89 was flown by Hubert Broad, at Hatfield, on 17 April 1934 as E4. This aircraft was eventually to be sold to the Ostschweiz Aero Geselschaft at St Gallen as CH-287, later to became HB-APA.

Production commenced at Hatfield with c/n 6250 and the type became known as the Dragon Rapide or, more commonly, just plain Rapide.

With the arrival of war, civil Rapides were impressed into RAF service and production was increased to provide the Dominie navigation and W/T trainers. In 1942 production was transferred to Loughborough to make way for Mosquito production. The total number of Rapides built reached 728 over a ten year period.

Post-war saw the Rapide being used worldwide as various fledgling airlines bought some of the surplus aircraft being disposed of by the services.

DH89 G-ACZE c/n 6264

Right: An early machine off the Hatfield production line 'CZE was built in 1934 and registered to the Anglo Persian Oil Co Ltd, and based at Abadan. It later returned to England and was sold to Airwork Ltd at Heston who operated it until the beginning of the war when it was impressed as Z7266 on 15 July 1940.

After a chequered career it crashed at Grimsetter, Orkney, on 27 December 1945. Struck off charge it was stored at Dyce, Aberdeen, until rebuilt by the DH Repair Unit at Witney. It was one of two Witney rebuilds and was given a new c/n of W1001 and re-registered as G-AJGS leading another chequered post-war career. The aircraft ended up being stored at Lakeview, New York, under the ownership of R. M. Schultz until discovered by Brian Woodford in 1984. Brian bought the aircraft and had it shipped to Ron Souch's workshops at Hamble for restoration. Registered to Brian's holding company 'Wessex Aviation and Transport Ltd', it regained its original marks as G-ACZE.

During the Thirties the Prince of Wales (later King Edward VIII) used two Rapides and 'CZE is painted to represent these aircraft with the Prince of Wales' feathers emblem on the fin.

The photograph was taken on 8 August 1987 with Peter Harrison at the controls.

DH89 G-ACZE

Below: The Prince of Wales Feathers adorn the fin of DH89 G-ACZE.

DH89 G-AGSH c/n 6884

Left: Rapide G-AGSH, formerly NR808 and EI-AJO, was built at Loughborough. Following disposal after the war 'GSH was converted to civil standard at de Havilland's Witney production line. Bought by BEAC it served on the various routes to the Channel Islands as 'Sir James Keir Hardie'.

Much later in its life the aircraft was owned by a Channel Islands-based group, one of whom, Peter Harrison, flew the aircraft for a photo session on 10 July 1981.

Below: Brian Woodford (right) owner of Rapide G-ACZE, Dragonfly G-AEDT and many others has the largest collection of de Havilland types in the world. Many of the aircraft are kept at his private strip at Chalmington, Dorset.

DH89 ZK-AKU

Overleaf: Part of the New Zealand Warbirds collection based at Dairy Flat airfield north of Auckland, Rapide ZK-AKU is finished in RNZAF marks as NZ528 and is pictured over the Whangaparoa peninsula on 9 February 1989.

DH89 ZK-AKU
Left: The Warbirds of New Zealand DH89 ZK-AKU banks
away from the late afternoon sun near its home base of Dairy
Flat north of Auckland on 9 February 1989.

Above: A view of the cockpit of DH89 ZK-AKY.

DH89 ZK-AKY

Above: Gerry Kluck flying DH89 ZK-AKY on a trip from
Waipukurau to Masterton, North Island, on 5 February 1989,
Named 'Tui' (Maori for Parson Bird) the aircraft is painted in
National Airways Corporation colours and is based at
Masterton.

DH90 DRAGONFLY

Although the DH90 Dragonfly followed on from the DH89 Dragon Rapide any similarity was purely superficial. The fuselage was a monocoque shell of preformed plywood with spruce stringers which was then covered with fabric as opposed to the plywood box, stringer and former construction of the DH84, '86 and '89.

Power was provided by two Gipsy Major 1/1C/1D/1O engines of between 130 and 145hp.

Struts and external bracing were reduced to a minimum to gain maximum performance from drag reduction. The main centre section of the wing consisted of a massive spar to take the engine and undercarriage loads and also housed two 30 gallon fuel tanks. A third fuel tank, carrying 25 gallons, was fitted in the rear of the cabin.

The prototype DH90, E2 (later G-ADNA), flew at Hatfield on 12 August 1935. Sixty seven examples of the DH90 were built in the c/n range 7500–7566.

This particular example, G-AEDT, is currently the only airworthy machine in the world although G-AEDU is undergoing an extensive rebuild for Torquil Norman after a severe landing accident at Clark County Airport, Indiana, on 22 September 1987.

'EDT was first registered, in June 1936, to Squadron Leader the Rt Hon Sir Philip Sassoon who was, at the time not only Honorary Air Commodore of 601 (County of London) Squadron RAuxAF, but also Secretary-of-State for Air. Based at Lympne airfield 'EDT remained with her first owner until 1938 when it was sold to Adastra Airways Pty Ltd, of Australia, and registered VH-AAD. Its main duty was aerial survey work which continued through the war years until 1951 when the aircraft was sold to Bush Pilots Pty Ltd. Further owners followed until, in 1963, it was purchased by Charles Masefield and Lord Trefgarne and flown to the UK arriving at London's Gatwick Airport on 23 December to regain its former registration marks.

During 1964 'EDT was flown across the Atlantic, via Prestwick, to be bought by the Tallmantz Collection of Santa Ana, California, as N2034. After passing into the hands of Rosen-Novak Autos of Omaha, it was bought by Joe Terteling of Glider Field, Boise, Idaho. Here it remained for 17 years deteriorating to a very poor condition until it was auctioned on 20 September 1986. The purchaser was Brian Woodford and the inevitable restorer was Ron Souch and his team at Hamble.

The wings were in reasonable shape but the only use for the fuselage was to be the pattern for an almost completely new fuselage. Most of the metal fittings and some of the spruce parts were incorporated into the new structure.

The first post restoration flight was made by Martin Barraclough, former owner of Dragonfly G-AEDU, and took place at RNAS Lee-on-Solent on 15 July 1988. The aircraft was finished in the blue and silver colours in which it appeared when owned by Sir Philip Sassoon.

The photographs reproduced here were taken during a sortie on 7 August 1988, whilst being flown by Peter Harrison.

DH90 G-AEDT c/n 7508

Right: 'EDT routeing along the south coast of England on a glorious summer's day on 7 August 1988.

Below: 601 Squadron Crest displayed on the fin of DH90 G-AEDT.

DH94 MOTH MINOR

Flight for 29 June 1939 stated that 'The object behind the particular layout of the Moth Minor' — 'may briefly be given as that of providing adequate performance at the lowest possible initial and later costs'. This was essentially the same goal for which the DH60 was produced. By the early thirties it was becoming plain the biplane layout was soon to be rather passé and that the future lay with the cantilever monoplane structure. 1931 brought the DH81 Swallow Moth, which was the first result of this thinking but, with the trade conditions prevailing at the time, the project was shelved, only one aircraft being built.

Some years later the idea was revived and another scheme for such an aircraft was proposed by Geoffrey de Havilland. This aircraft was to be an all-wood, tandem seat, tailwheel type with a 90hp Gipsy Minor engine designed by Major Halford. Construction was similar to that in the DH60 and the aircraft was designed around a sturdy centre section made up of two box spars, braced at each end by a pair of ribs. This centre section carried the two undercarriage legs, two control column mountings, the front seat and the fuel tanks. One of the two tanks could be removed to create extra luggage space. A perforated air brake was hinged to the underside of the rear spar to steepen the glide.

The fuselage consisted of four longerons with dividing bulkheads and, covered with plywood, was glued and bolted to the centre section.

Attached to the ends of the centre section were the folding wings which were built around two spars and were covered with ply forward of the rear spar, the rest being fabric covered. The differential ailerons and tail surfaces were also fabric covered.

The first flight of the prototype, E-4, was made at Hatfield by Captain de Havilland on 22 June 1937. By June 1939 Moth Minor production had reached eight per week and the ex-factory price was £575.

After 103 Moth Minors had been built at Hatfield, production was stopped early in 1940 to make way for war production. All the drawings, tools and jigs were shipped to Australia where a production line was set up at Bankstown to provide an interim training aircraft until the DH82A production could be increased.

DH94 G-AFOB c/n 94018
Left: DH94 Moth Minor G-AFOB taxies in at its home base at Chalmington, Dorset. 'FOB is part of collector, Brian Woodford's, collection of DH types.

DH94 ZK-AKM/NZ597 c/n 94012
Overleaf: This aircraft was a Hatfield-built aircraft, G-AFON, which was delivered to the London Aeroplane Club but was sold on to New Zealand via Australia to fly with the New Plymouth Aero Club as ZK-AHK. With the coming of war all private flying was stopped and 'AHK was impressed into RNZAF service as NZ597 with No.22 Squadron. After the war she was re-registered ZK-AKM and flew in numerous hands until acquired by a group at Dairy Flat, Auckland. There have been a few engine problems but those seem to be ironed out now and the aircraft was put in the air by Stan Smith, with his wife Jill along for the ride, on 9 February 1989 for a photo session.

DH98 MOSQUITO

'Why is your bomber so big and slow?'
'Because of the weight of all the defensive guns and gunners it has
to carry!'
'Why carry all those guns and gunners?'
'Because it's so big and slow!'

The development of the bomber in the '20s and '30s was, with but few exceptions, lagging behind that of the fighters. Fighters had to have a high performance in order to reach their natural prey. As a result the slower bomber had to carry defensive armament. This meant carrying gunners to operate the armament, with all their associated equipment. The aircraft's weight grew and it flew more slowly. This demanded more power. This increased fuel consumption, reducing range. More fuel had to be carried. More power was needed. Designers and military men were caught in a vicious circle.

The origins of the DH98 can be traced back to the London–Melbourne race of 1934. The winner, as already recounted, was the DH88, G-ACSS, flown by C. W. A. Scott and Tom Campbell Black. Curiously, though, it was the DC-2 flown by Captain K. D. Parmentier which came second which caused de Havilland to make representations to the British Government to try to convince them that the UK was falling seriously behind the USA in airliner development. DH proposed that the government should help to finance an airliner which could compete with the designs starting to come out of the American factories. This aircraft would be made of wood, along the lines of the DH88 and it would be powered by four Gipsy King engines. Each engine was, essentially, two cylinder blocks from a Gipsy Six mounted on a common crankcase.

Eventually, on 21 January 1936, the Air Ministry placed an order for two prototypes of the DH91 Albatross, arguably one of the most aesthetically pleasing piston-engined airliners ever built.

Development and construction preceded apace and the first flight of the prototype, with Class 'B' marks 'E2', took place on 20 May 1937 at Hatfield in the hands of R. J. Waight.

The fuselage was different to that of the DH88 as it had a stressed skin structure consisting of two layers of cedar plywood with a layer of balsa between. These were cemented, under pressure, on a retractable jig. The wing was a one-piece cantilever structure of 105 feet span built around a box spar. Provision for the four Gipsy Kings was made as were wheel wells for the retractable tail wheel undercarriage.

Seven aircraft were built. Imperial Airways had two versions — one to carry mail and the other carried 22 passengers and four crew. January 2 1939 saw the inauguration of services from Croydon to Paris, Brussels and Zurich. The efficiency of these aircraft, cruising at 210mph, was most impressive.

By 1938 Hitler had been in power in Germany for five years and rearmament in Europe was well under way. De Havillands were looking at ways to help Britain and one of the projects for discussion was a bomber version of the DH91 Albatross. As it stood it could carry 6,000lbs of bombs to Berlin at 210mph. But not all of the available space was required so a new fuselage was suggested. This would cut down the weight and increase the speed. As the weight was less a smaller wing could be used. With the smaller wing four engines seemed impractical so two engines were suggested instead but still giving the same power as the four Gipsy Kings. The Rolls Royce Merlin was the obvious choice as it was already powering the Hurricanes and Spitfires then coming in to service. A liquid-cooled V-12 it was giving 1,200hp and further development to higher power was already taking place.

Calculations showed that the performance of the aircraft was going to be of a very high order indeed and it was decided, on 29 December 1939, to omit all defensive armament and rely on the aircraft's speed to keep it out of trouble. A very bold decision at the time. With future development in mind provision was made in the underside of the nose section for four 20mm cannon for a planned fighter version.

Specification B1/40 was written round the new aircraft. The name Mosquito was considered appropriate as it retained the entomological names used in the Moth series and it stung unexpectedly.

As Hatfield was considered vulnerable to enemy attack the technical offices were moved to Salisbury Hall at London Colney a few miles from Hatfield. Here the prototype Mosquito, with Class 'B' registration E-0234, took shape under the direction of R. E. Bishop, that promising young man who joined the company in 1921 and who became Chief Designer after Arthur Hagg's resignation in 1937. The DH98s wing was designed by R. A. Tamblin.

Getting this far was not easy in the face of official reluctance to proceed with the project but de Havilland convinced Sir Wilfrid Freeman of the Air Council that it should go ahead and it was he who championed the Mosquito in official circles. Indeed the aircraft became known as 'Freeman's Folly'. A lesser man might have given in against such opposition.

In 1940 Lord Beaverbrook was appointed Minister of Aircraft Production and, because of the dire position that Britain was now in, slowed all work on projects which would not provide any immediate operational benefits. As the Mosquito was about 18 months away from being

DH98 Mosquito T.III RR299/G-ASKH

Overleaf: Built at Leavesden in March 1945 RR299 was one of a batch of 50 Mosquitos ordered in the serial range RR270–319. She was completed as a T.III dual control trainer. After 1,107 hours 50 minutes flying time '299 was retired to 27 MU on 14 March 1963. The aircraft was acquired by Hawker Siddeley Aviation on 10 July 1963 and registered as G-ASKH two days later. She now flies regularly at air displays around the country.

The photograph here was taken on a flight from Wyton to Bournemouth on 17 July 1983, with BAe test pilot Tony Craig in command.

operational it was included in these cuts. C. G. Long of the design staff managed to demonstrate to Lord Beaverbrook that the Mosquito was using hardly any strategic materials or manpower and that great benefits would accrue if the development could continue. The project was reinstated in July on condition that it did not interfere with work of immediate importance.

The yellow painted prototype was built in great secrecy at Salisbury Hall and then transported to Hatfield on 3 November 1940. Less than eleven months after design work had started the first Mosquito took to the air on 25 November 1940 in the hands of Geoffrey de Havilland Jnr with John E. Walker, the engine installation designer, as observer. Performance was nothing short of incredible for a twin-engined bomber. Everyone knew that they had a war-winning aircraft.

The development potential for the aircraft was tremendous and Fighter, Night Fighter, Bomber, Reconnaissance and Pathfinder versions were all proposed and developed. Variants for anti shipping strike using 60 lbs rockets were built. A version using the bouncing bomb codenamed 'Highball' was developed but never used for fear that the Germans might copy the idea. It was intended that the battleship 'Tirpitz' would be the subject of this weapon's attentions. Other versions could carry the monster 4,000 lbs bomb. It can be said that the Mosquito was the first true Multi Role Combat Aircraft.

Early development showed very few real snags but one which did cause a design change was the lengthening of the engine nacelles as the short nacelles caused higher drag than expected and they appeared to contribute to flutter of the tail surfaces. The prototype became W4050 when brought under the standard RAF serial system. This aircraft still exists today at the Mosquito museum at Salisbury Hall.

The first three Mosquitos to enter RAF service were W4051, 4054 and 4055. The first operational sortie was by W4055 on 20 September 1941 on a PR sortie over the harbours at Brest and Bordeaux.

By May 1942 the RAF were operating bomber and fighter versions of this magnificent aircraft which was confounding its critics by proving that the high speed unarmed concept worked and worked extremely well. The Luftwaffe were finding it very difficult to intercept the Mossie.

First official public acknowledgement of the Mosquito was made after the destruction of Gestapo HQ in Oslo on 26 November 1942. This was the first of the 'set piece' low-level daylight raids that were to help make the name Mosquito famous around the world.

Another spectacular attack, this time on the Shellhaus building in Copenhagen, took place on 21 March 1945 with aircraft from 21 Squadron, 464 Squadron and 487 Squadron escorted by Mustangs of 64 Squadron. Danish resistance leaders believed that the Gestapo were about to make mass arrests and requested that their HQ be destroyed. This was done. Records were destroyed and many Gestapo agents were killed. Aircraft were flying so low that one flown by Wing Commander Kleboe, crashed into a flagpole. Unfortunately one aircraft crashed into a school with considerable loss of life. The Danes accepted this as part of the price they had to pay for freedom.

A similar raid was carried out on 17 April 1945 by six aircraft on a school building in Odense which was occupied by the Gestapo.

In January 1944 the French Resistance notified London that more than 100 Frenchmen were awaiting execution in Amiens prison for helping Allied airmen to escape. Could the RAF break down the walls of the prison and get them out?

Operation 'Jericho', as it was most appropriately called, was put in the hands of Group Captain Basil Embry to organise.

Aircraft of 487 Squadron would lead with 21 and 464 Squadrons supporting. Escort was to be provided by the Typhoons of 198 Squadron.

Nineteen Mosquitos took off from Hunsdon in a snowstorm on 18 February 1944. Four got detached from the main formation and returned to base. Twelve Typhoons took off but four of their number returned to base.

Detailed planning for the raid called for the breaching of the prison walls first. Then the guards quarters were to be destroyed followed by the breaching of the walls of the building itself.

Two hundred and fifty eight of the 700 prisoners escaped, twelve were to have been shot the following day. One hundred and two inmates were killed in the bombing or shot by the guards whilst escaping. Some civilian helpers were also killed.

Casualties were expected and accepted. Most of the prisoners would have been executed. Despite the deaths the RAF, with the Mosquito, saved many lives that day.

The whole operation was filmed by an aircraft of the Film Production Unit which orbited the area for seven minutes taking cine and still film of the event, despite the presence of FW190s sent up to intercept. It too was a Mosquito.

One pilot making his mark on history at this time was Wing Commander John Cunningham who, with his navigator Jimmy Rawnsley, was to be nominated the most outstanding night fighter pilot of the war by the 'Official History of the Second World War'. John Cunningham rose to be Chief Test Pilot of the Aircraft Company when Geoffrey de Havilland Jnr was killed in the DH108 accident over the Thames estuary near Gravesend on 27 September 1946. He was subsequently to make the first flight of that most attractive of jet airliners the Comet on 27 July 1949.

The operations undertaken by the Mosquito were many and varied, photo reconnaissance — both high and low level; radar-equipped night fighters; long range escort fighter; ground attack with bombs, cannons and rockets; low-level pinpoint attacks such as those on the various Gestapo HQs; anti-shipping and U-boat strikes using the Molins 57 mm gun; pathfinders for the RAF's 'Heavies' using aids such as 'Oboe', 'G-H' and 'H2S' to drop Target Indicators. 'Highball' operations were developed although, in the event, were not carried out. The 4,000 lb bomb carried by some Mosquitos was the same as the whole bomb load carried by the B-17! That aircraft was slower, more vulnerable and, if shot down, nine crew were lost to the war effort rather than the two of the Mosquitos.

Mosquitos were built at Hatfield, Leavesden and Chester by de Havilland, also by the Standard Motor Company, Airspeed Ltd at Christchurch, Hampshire and the Percival Aircraft Co at Luton. Licence production took place by de Havilland (Canada) at Downsview, Ontario and by de Havilland (Australia) at Bankstown, Sydney. Production of all variants ceased after 7,781 aircraft.

DH100 VAMPIRE

Developments, in the late '30s and the early '40s, of the jet engine, by Frank Whittle, were beginning to show promise but funding was on a shoestring budget. Early in 1941 discussion within the de Havilland company centred around the possibility of building a turbo jet engine and also a fighter type aircraft to be powered by it. The resulting engine was the Goblin with a centrifugal compressor and was designed by Frank Halford. The airframe which was designed around the Goblin was built to specification E6/41 and was named the DH100 Spider Crab. This name was soon abandoned in favour of the Vampire. The Goblin engine ran for the first time on 13 April 1942 and the go ahead for the Vampire was given in May 1942.

The initial Goblin 1 gave a thrust of 2,700lbs st as installed in the prototype aircraft. The developed Goblin 2 gave 3,100lbs st.

The engine/cockpit nacelle was of wooden construction and it was built using similar methods to those adopted for the Mosquito. The wings, tailplane and tailbooms were of metal construction.

The first prototype, LZ548/G was taken aloft for the first time on 29 September 1943 at Hatfield in the hands of Geoffrey de Havilland Jnr. The third prototype, MP838/G, was the first to be fitted with the standard armament of four 20mm Hispano cannon. An order was placed on 13 May 1944 for an initial batch of 120 Vampire Mk1s. These were to be built by the English Electric Co at Preston. The first production aircraft flew at Samlesbury on 20 April 1945.

DH100 Vampire Mk6

Shortly after the end of the Second World War the Swiss Air Force decided to evaluate various types of turbo-jet powered fighters to replace the Me109s then in service. Even at that early date it was realised that the jet fighter had the potential to be developed to a far higher performance level than the piston-engined fighters then in service and the Swiss Air Force wanted the best aircraft available to protect the country's neutrality.

During the summer of 1946 a purchasing commission visited Hatfield to study the DH100 Vampire Mk1. Following this visit three aircraft were ordered for evaluation in the Swiss environment. These aircraft were given the serials J-1001 to J-1003. Unfortunately J-1001 (ex RAF TG433) was written off in a take-off accident on 2 August 1946. A fourth aircraft

NE PAS POUSSER
NICHT STOSSEN

Ae. A. 6467
Ae. A. 6468 a

J-1178

was obtained as a replacement and given the serial J-1004. These aircraft remained in service until retired in 1961.

After the evaluation period an order was placed, during 1948, with de Havillands for 75 aircraft. These were to Mk6 standard and all were built in England, at Hatfield and Chester. Serials were allotted in the range J-1005 to J-1079 and the first was delivered in May 1949. These aircraft remained in service until 1971. One example, J-1068, can still be seen in the Swiss Transport Museum at Lucerne.

A further order, for 100 aircraft, was also placed but these were to be built under licence, in Switzerland, by the Swiss Federal Aircraft at Emmen, Flug und Fahrzeugwerke AG of Altenrhein and Pilatus Flugzeugwerke AG of Stans.

The first of these was delivered in 1951 and the batch was allotted the serial range J-1101 to J-1201. In 1960 a further three aircraft were constructed from spares and given serials J-1080 to J-1082.

In 1960 this batch was modified to accept a Martin Baker ejection seat. This resulted in a revised cockpit canopy.

The Swiss Air Force still operate a considerable number of Vampires in the advanced training role as pilots transition from the Pilatus PC-7 to the Hunters, Mirages and F-5Es of the front line units. These aircraft are expected to retire from service as the Air Force takes delivery of the BAe Hawk in 1990.

Some Vampires have been fitted with Target Towing apparatus and are painted in a striking orange and black striped scheme. These aircraft are being replaced with Pilatus PC-9s leased from the manufacturer.

In 1954 the first of 150 licence-built DH112 Venom Mk1s entered service.

The acquisition of all these, for the time, high performance aircraft led to inevitable problems with pilot conversion. To ease these problems, DH115 Trainers were ordered in various batches. The first three were delivered, by the Swiss Federal Aircraft Factory, using British-built fuselages, in 1953. Seven more were delivered commencing in 1956 and a further batch of twenty followed in 1958. The first ten aircraft were in the serial range U-1001 to U-1010 but after 1 June 1957 they were allocated new serials sequentially from U-1201 to U-1230.

In 1967 the need arose for a further batch of airframes and these fell available from ex RAF stocks. Nine aircraft were transported, by road, to Altenrhein for overhaul prior to entering service. Serials were U-1231 to U-1239.

DH100 Vampire FB6 J-1178
Left: Pictured under a brilliant blue Alpine sky Vampire J-1178 is framed by another Vampire at the Swiss Air Force training base at Sion in October 1987. Over 40 years after the first Vampire flew with the Swiss Air Force the type is now about to be replaced by the BAe Hawk in the advanced training role for pilots streaming on to the Hunters, F-5Es, Mirages and, soon, the F-18s used to defend the country's neutrality.

DH100 Vampire FB6 J-1003/J-1006

Previous page: Flown by Jean-Marie Frachebourg and Robert Schubiger, both Swissair captains on their annual militia service, these two Vampire FB6s were shot on 4 October 1988 near Emmen. Fitted for the target towing role these aircraft are only now about to be replaced by the Pilatus PC-9 and will have been in service for 40 years on their retirement.

DH100 and DH115 Vampires

Below: Photographed at their Sion base are lines of Swiss Air Force Vampires awaiting their next sorties. Assigned to the operational training role the Vampires are now being phased out of service, commencing 1990, as deliveries of the BAe Hawk are made.

DH115 Vampire U-1233
Below: Photographed during an air-to-air sortie from Emmen near Lucerne is DH115 U-1233. This is one of nine ex-RAF machines purchased in 1967 and transported by road to Altenrhein to be overhauled by FFA for the Swiss Air Force.

DH100 Vampire FB6 J-1191
Overleaf: Shot on a sortie from Sion, in October 1987, over the Swiss Alps near Mont Blanc.

DH104 DOVE

With the cessation of hostilities in Europe de Havilland's attentions turned back to the civil airline market. Some time before the end of the war the Brabazon Committee sat to give consideration as to what types of aircraft would be required to get the civil market back on its feet. One of the types proposed was a modern replacement for the DH89 Dragon Rapide. Because of their pre-war success with the Rapide, and the DH84 Dragon, de Havilland decided this was one of the projects they should tackle.

The DH104 was an all-metal low wing cantilever monoplane with a semi-monocoque fuselage and was the first all-metal aircraft tackled since the pre-war DH95 Flamingo. Power was to be provided by two Gipsy Queen 70 engines of 330 hp. The tricycle undercarriage was pneumatically retractable.

Typical performance figures for the Dove 1B and 2B were an a.u.w. of 8,500 lbs cruising speed of 179 mph and a maximum speed of 210 mph.

The first prototype, G-AGPJ, was flown by Geoffrey Pike at Hatfield on 25 September 1945 on the 25th anniversary of the founding of the Company.

DH104 Sea Devon C20 G-NAVY c/n 04406
Left: Originally a civil Dove 6 G-AMXX, this aircraft was bought by the Royal Navy as XJ348 and ended its service days with 721 Squadron at Lee-on-Solent. On its retirement the aircraft was bought by John Flavell and Ken Fehrenbach to be based at Shoreham with the new registration G-NAVY. It is seen here being flown by John Flavell on 2 September 1982.

DH106 COMET

During the Second World War Lord Brabazon of Tara chaired a committee convened to determine the future shape of the British aircraft industry in terms of the types of aircraft required for the civil market. Various types were specified to suit different operations and manufacturers sought to design and build these types which, hopefully, would put Britain in the forefront of civil aviation again. Successful aircraft spawned by the committee were the Bristol Britannia, Vickers Viscount and the de Havilland Dove. Not so successful were the Miles Marathon and Brabazon itself.

In the USA the C-54 from Douglas, the Lockheed C-89 and the C-97 (itself derived from the B-29 bomber) were all being developed for the US military and had obvious applications as post-war civil airliners. All were piston-engined aircraft but could take the civil market by storm, if allowed to.

Geoffrey de Havilland, himself a member of the Brabazon Committee, realised that the future lay with the gas turbine powered aircraft and proposed that de Havilland design and build a jet transport. This emerged as the 'Brabazon Type IV'.

At this time (mid–late 1944) no one really knew what a jet powered airliner ought to look like and various schemes were proposed. One looked like a scaled up DH100, another had a canard foreplane with the engines in a cluster at the rear, yet another was a tailless design. The latter idea seemed good and this was seriously pursued for a time. All posed problems of one kind or another.

As finally presented the new DH106 was fairly conventional in general layout although it had many features of very advanced design and thinking for its time.

The four Ghost 50s chosen to power it were buried in the wing roots with access doors for servicing. The cabin air system could pressurise the hull to $8\frac{1}{4}$lbs/ins^2 differential to give a cabin altitude of 8,000 feet at 40,000 feet. This in itself was an amazing technical feat. Pressurisation and airframe deicing were achieved using air bled from the centrifugal compressor of the Ghost engines.

With the fall of Germany, the research that their scientists had been carrying out into swept wings became available and de Havilland used this to advantage on the DH106 although they trod carefully in this new area and the Comet had only moderate sweepback on the wing leading edge and almost none on the trailing edge. The main undercarriage of the Comet prototype consisted of a single large mainwheel on each side but on subsequent aircraft this became the now familiar four wheel bogie arrangement, another de Havilland first. The hydraulic systems, the electrical systems, Redux bonding, tricycle undercarriages and power controls were all in their infancy. De Havilland brought them all together, with a new form of propulsion, in an aircraft that could fly twice as fast and twice as high as any before it bar the early jet fighters.

In order that de Havilland could study the effects of swept wings at high speeds the DH108 research aircraft was built using a Vampire nacelle with a new wing and no tail. It was experience with this aircraft that led to the decision that the Comet must have a tail.

Detailed design of what was to emerge as the beautifully graceful shape of the Comet began in the summer of 1945 and led to the first flight of the prototype, G-5-1, later G-ALVG, on 27 July 1949 in the hands of John Cunningham, now chief test pilot since Geoffrey de Havilland Jnr had been killed in the breakup of a DH108 over the Thames estuary.

Many route-proving flights were carried out to many destinations showing the world Britain's lead in aviation. Because of the performance of the Comet every one of these flights broke one record or another. De Havilland, the Comet and Britain were head and shoulders above the rest of the world with their achievements.

DH106 Comet C4 G-BDIW

Below: Framed by the fin of another Comet, ex RAF Comet C4 G-BDIW awaits its next passenger load during the summer of 1980. This particular Comet was destined to operate the type's last revenue service with Dan Air on 9 November 1980.

BOAC ordered ten Comet 1s and services commenced, with fare-paying passengers, on 2 May 1952 to Johannesburg.

The new aircraft was not without its problems though, and a couple of aircraft were lost due to the phenomenon of 'Ground Stall' where, if rotated to too high an angle of attack on take off the wing stalled. The drag became too high, the aircraft could not accelerate to lift off speed. Conversely the speed was then too high to abandon take off within the available runway distance remaining. The first overrun disaster happened at Rome and the second at Karachi. Modification of the wing leading edges prevented a recurrence.

The worst incidents were the three aircraft lost in mysterious circumstances, one out of Calcutta and two out of Rome, near Elba and Stromboli. All three aircraft crashed into the sea making discovery of the problem extremely difficult. The Comet was grounded.

A massive effort was made to retrieve Comet G-ALYP from the Mediterranean near Elba and, in an amazing piece of detective work by the Accident Investigation Branch at Farnborough, the airframe was painstakingly pieced back together and the problem found. A fatigue failure near an ADF hatch had led to an explosive decompression of the fuselage leading to an almost instantaneous breakup of the Comet. Having discovered the cause the solution was fairly simple and all hatches were given well radiussed corners and all the square windows were turned into elipses to prevent stress concentrations at sharp corners. The problem was solved but the Comet was tarnished.

The first few Comets were built at Hatfield but later production was split between Hatfield and Chester. Development led to the Comet 2 series with Rolls Royce Avons and then on, via the sole Comet 3, to the Comets 4, 4B and 4C with higher power Avons.

Comets were bought by many of the world's airlines including BOAC, Air France, BEA, United Arab Airlines (later Egyptair), Mexicana and Olympic Airways. They also saw service with the RAF. The world's first Trans-Atlantic jet services were operated by the Comet carrying fare-paying passengers on 4 October 1958. Two aircraft flew simultaneous opposite direction services with BOAC. During the following month all BOACs Trans-Atlantic services were operated by the Comet 4 and further services were added as aircraft came off the production line.

The last civil Comets were operated by Dan Air which had the largest fleet of all, using the Comet 4, 4B and 4C as well as the retired RAF C4s. The last commercial service took place at Gatwick on 9 November 1980, using the one-time RAF Comet C4 G-BDIW.

Two Comets still fly. One, XV814, is operated by the RAE at Farnborough. This aircraft was formerly G-APDF, a Comet 4, with BOAC. The other is XS235 with the A&AEE at Boscombe Down. The Comet lives on, however, in a much modified form as it was to be the basis for the RAF's Maritime Patrol aircraft — the Nimrod. Engined now with Rolls Royce Speys this Comet derivative will serve the RAF for many years to come.

The man who gave the world jet travel in the shape of its first jet airliner was the designer R. E. Bishop. As recounted earlier, he joined DH at Stag Lane in 1921 and was later to design, amongst other types, the Mosquito. For that alone he deserves great recognition but his crowning glory was that most graceful of jet airliners — the Comet 4C.

R. E. Bishop died on 11 June 1989, aged 86, shortly before the 40th anniversary of the first Comet flight.

DH106 Comet 4C XS235 c/n 6473
Left: Photographed on 9 July 1991 Comet 4C, XS235, is one of only two Comets which are airworthy today.

DH112 VENOM

Continued development of the DH Goblin turbojet led to the DH Ghost increasing the thrust from 3,100lbs st to 4,850lbs st on the Ghost 103 and even higher on later versions.

To take advantage of this increase in thrust de Havilland designed a new fighter which, superficially, resembled the earlier DH100 Vampire. Much of the difference lay in the design of the wing. The aerofoil section was much thinner and the wing had a slight sweep-back on the leading edge with a straight trailing edge. These features permitted a higher Mach number to be attained before compressibility problems set in. Jettisonable tip tanks were a standard fit and were a recognition feature. A tendency to tip stall at low speeds required the use of wing fences mid way between the booms and the tips.

The first Venom, VV612, flew at Hatfield on 2 September 1949. Armament consisted of four 20mm Hispano cannon in the nose and the aircraft could carry 2,000lbs of bombs or eight rocket projectiles under the wings.

Many countries which had operated the Vampire were queuing for the Venom. One of those countries was Switzerland which built 150 Venom FB 1s and 100 FB 4s under licence. The Ghost engine was also built in Switzerland by Sulzer Freres of Winterthur. The FB 1s were in the serial range J-1501 to J-1650. The aircraft J-1626 to J-1649 were adapted to the photo reconnaissance role and were fitted with underwing PR pods and designated DH112 Mk1Rs.

The 100 FB 4s were in the serial range J-1701 to J-1800. The last Venoms were retired in 1984 after some 30 years continuous service. Some found their way to the civil market and others into museums such as the Air Force museum at Dubendorf.

DH112 G-GONE c/n 752

Left: Owned by John Davies and Phil Meeson G-GONE was retired from the Swiss Air Force in 1984. Powered by a Ghost 48 the aircraft was in service as J-1542 showing it to be a Venom FB 1.

After a display at Hatfield on 1 July 1989 John intercepted the camera plane high over the Isle of Wight for a photo session before returning to the aircraft's base at Bournemouth (Hurn). Seen here in spurious Royal Navy marks it is expected that the aircraft will be repainted in its original Swiss Air Force marks, if permission is granted by the Swiss authorities.

DH112 Venom J-1753

Right: The Venom is no longer operational with the Swiss Air Force although a few are flying in private hands. This example, J-1753, has now found a permanent home in the Swiss Air Force Museum at Dubendorf on the outskirts of Zurich where it is displayed with a range of its armament.

DH114 HERON

The DH114 was what we would nowadays refer to as a 'stretch' of a basic design. Modern manufacturers do it to their aircraft to extend their product range and to cut down development costs. De Havilland took the DH104 Dove, kept the outer wing panels, the nose and tail units and added two more engines, new fuselage sections and a new wing centre section and the DH114 was born. Construction methods were, naturally, the same and two pilots and 17 passengers could be carried aloft on the power of four Gipsy Queen 30s of 250hp. This engine in developed form eventually delivered 340hp.

Detail design began in 1949 under W. A. Tamblin and the prototype, c/n 10903, took to the air as G-ALZL at Hatfield on 10 May 1950. Construction numbers were allocated in the 14001 block for production aircraft. C/ns 14001–14007 were Heron 1s built at Hatfield and 14008–14099 were built at Chester. The Heron 1 was easily distinguishable from the Heron 2 as it had a fixed undercarriage. Airframe 14006 acted as the prototype Heron 2 the line for which was also at Chester.

Herons are now a rare species but four were operational with 'Heron Flight' at RNAS Yeovilton, Somerset, until December 1989.

DH114 Sea Heron C.Mk20 XR445 c/n 14092

Below: Prior to its re-equipment with BAe Jetstream aircraft the Heron Flight, at RNAS Yeovilton (HMS Heron in Navy circles), operated a small fleet of Herons. The aircraft were finally retired from service in December 1989.

This particular example, XR445, was photographed over the Solent, near Portsmouth, on 2 November 1988.

DH114 Heron C.4 XM296 c/n 14130

Previous page and right: XM296 was a Chester-built airframe and was delivered, with XM295, to the Queen's Flight at RAF Benson during 1958. With the arrival of HS 748s, in 1972, the Heron was transferred to the Fleet Air Arm at RNAS Yeovilton, Somerset. Now in service with the Navy it continued its previous role as a VIP transport being used to transport the Flag Officer Naval Air Command, other Naval VIPs and guests of the Navy. Having been resident at Yeovilton for so long it is now affectionately referred to as 'The Barge'.

   Due to retire from active duty December 1989, having amassed 10,200 hours over 31 years, a photo sortie was arranged on 12 October 1989. Crew for the occasion was Lt Cmdr Tom Mason and CPO Paul Newman. The chosen location was over the eastern end of the Isle of Wight at 4,500 feet.

DHC 1 EC-BOI

Left: Operated by Jose Chicharro Villar, Chipmunk EC-BOI is based at Gerona, Spain, and was photographed on 31 July 1987.

DHC 1 G-AOSZ c/n C1/0080

Below: Peter Villa and John Pothecary flying Chipmunk G-AOSZ near Shoreham on 3 August 1981. The aircraft appears in the BIA colours because Peter Villa was the Managing Director of British Island Airways.

DHC 1 CHIPMUNK

One man that was to have a profound effect on the fortunes of de Havilland (Canada) was a Pole, Wsiewolod J. Jakimiuk. Jakimiuk had been Chief Engineer at the National Aircraft Factory in Poland and had designed PZL fighters before the German invasion on 1 September 1939. Under an arrangement with the Polish government in exile he managed to get to Canada, with others, and to work for de Havillands at Downsview. Much good work was done during the war years with wartime production but 'Jaki' was looking further ahead and, in 1943, thoughts were turning to a new low wing tandem seater primary trainer.

Summer of 1945 saw Francis St Barbe at Downsview discussing post-war projects with Managing Director Phil Garratt. St Barbe saw Jakimiuk's model of the new trainer on Garratt's desk and realised that this could be the new trainer for the world market to replace the Tiger Moth.

By October 1945 design work was well under way and two prototypes were authorised on the 31st of the month.

It was decided that future de Havilland products from Canada would be named after Canadian animals and this first aircraft was named the Chipmunk and was to become one of the most delightful to fly trainers in the world with excellent control harmony, response and lightness of touch.

The DHC 1 Chipmunk had an all-metal stressed skin fuselage with a built up wing consisting of a single spar with a stressed skin leading edge D-box. The rest of the wing was fabric covered. The metal-framed flaps, ailerons, rudders and elevators were also fabric covered. Power was provided by a Gipsy Major of 145hp.

The first flight of the prototype was to have been carried out by Geoffrey de Havilland Jnr but, as he was busy dealing with events in England, Pat Fillingham was designated pilot and took CF-DIO X into the air for an hour on 22 May 1946.

The Chipmunk saw service in many of the world's air forces. Canadian production reached 218 aircraft but it was in the UK where most aircraft were built numbering 111 at Hatfield and 889 at Chester, with a further 60 in Portugal.

With the replacement of more modern aircraft many Chipmunks have been filtering on to the civil market in recent years.

DHC 1 G-BPAL/WG350

Left: Pete Kynsey flies for the camera whilst owner Richard Parker looks on from his Chipmunk G-BPAL, near Denham on 26 September 1987.

DHC 1 WG350/G-BPAL

Right: Under a stormy sky the camera catches Chipmunk G-BPAL in a patch of sunlight near Denham on 26 September 1987.

DHC 1 CF-URN/18073

Below: DHC 1 Chipmunks operated by the RCAF differed in various respects from their British-built counterparts. The most obvious difference lay with the use of a bubble type canopy. Here, a Canadian-built Chipmunk, CF-URN awaits its annual maintenance at Watt Martin's strip near Milton, Ontario, during May 1989.

143

DHC-2 BEAVER

Although the pre-war Fox Moth had been put back into production after the war, using surplus DH82C parts, as the DH83C, this was really only a short-term measure to keep the factory open and to provide the Bush operators with a usable aircraft. Everyone knew that the days of the DH83C were limited and that a purpose-designed, rugged, cheap and efficient aircraft was required.

Many of the strips and lakes which the operators flew into and out of were rather 'tight' so short take off and landing capability was required. (The concept of STOL as an operational technique can be said to have been born with the Beaver.) Half ton loads were the yardstick for sizing the aircraft. Around these requirements grew a rugged, all-metal, high wing aircraft with a high-aspect ratio, slotted flaps and a powerful engine.

It was originally planned that the engine would be a Gipsy Queen 50 of 295–330hp but various elements within DHC militated against this choice in favour of the more powerful P&W R-985 Wasp Junior of 450hp. The advocates of higher power won the day and the P&W engine was chosen with minimal redesign of the aircraft.

Being designed as an aerial truck, the Beaver featured high aspect ratio wings, long span slotted flaps and drooping ailerons to achieve the STOL behaviour so essential to the success of the design. The wings had hefty strut bracing and there was an immensely strong undercarriage to cope with the loads expected in service. There were two doors at the front of the aircraft and two at the rear which could be easily removed to carry awkward and bulky freight. Accommodation was for one pilot with three passengers on seats plus three more at the back on a hammock seat. All seats, except of course for the pilot's, were easily removable to carry freight for which a strong load-bearing floor was fitted. Fuel tanks were housed under the floor. All controls were kept very simple. Even the hydraulics for the flaps were hand pumped.

Russ Bannock took the first Beaver, CF-FHB-X into the air on 16 August 1947.

The bush operators loved the aircraft but so did the military and the US forces bought more than half of the total production of 1,629, as L-20s, where they saw service in many areas including Vietnam and Korea.

DHC-2 Beaver
Right: Aquaticair is a small Australian floatplane operator
using two DHC-2 Beavers and a GAF Nomad on short sectors
along the coast around Sydney. One of the airline's Beavers is
seen here shortly after arrival at the Palm Beach base a few
miles north of Sydney during February 1989.

DHC-2 ZK-CKH/NZ6001

Above: Based at Ardmore, near Auckland, New Zealand, this Beaver is part of the New Zealand Warbirds Group and is painted to represent one of the aircraft used by the New Zealand Antarctic Survey in the late 1950s.

DHC-3 OTTER

The only 'problem' with the DHC-2 Beaver was that it was designed as a 'half ton truck'. Inevitably there will always be somebody who wants more, so de Havilland (Canada) designers sat down and designed a 'one ton truck' just for those people.

Known early in the project stage as the 'King Beaver' design work was commenced on 29 November 1950. It was to carry twice the payload, have 2½ times the cabin volume and have a similar performance to the Beaver. Power was to be provided by a P&W R-1340 radial engine of 600 hp. Construction was generally similar to that of the Beaver although the King Beaver's fuselage was rounder than the box section of the Beaver.

Now designated the DHC-3 Otter the first flight of the new design was 12 December 1951 in the hands of George Neal. DHC now had a good product range and sales were extremely good of all types. Total sales of the Otter amounted to 466 which included many to operators of the Beaver. One new operator was the RCAF. They were one of the people who said that the DHC-2 was too small for them. The US Forces bought Otters and it became one of the world's earliest STOL airliners with airlines such as Philippine Airlines using them in and out of remote, small airstrips.

DH51 G-EBIR c/n 102
Below: Basking in the early evening sunset at Old Warden is
the Shuttleworth Collection's DH51 G-EBIR in the summer of
1987.